F

FEMININE
FUSION

CHRIS GRISCOM

A FIRESIDE BOOK
Published by Simon & Schuster
New York London Toronto
Sydney Tokyo Singapore

FIRESIDE
Simon & Schuster Building
Rockefeller Center
1230 Avenue of the Americas
New York, New York 10020

Designed by Black Angus Design Group
Manufactured in the United States of America

10 9 8 7 6 5 4 3 2 1

Library of Congress Cataloging in Publication Data
Griscom, Chris, date
    Feminine fusion / Chris Griscom.
        p.   cm.
    "A Fireside book."
    1. Sex differences (Psychology)   2. Femininity (Psychology)
I. Title.
    BF692.2.G75   1991
    155.3'33—dc20   91-27409
                                                  CIP

ISBN: 0-671-70844-9

This book is dedicated to
the Divine Feminine within us all.

Special acknowledgment must go to Barbara Gess for her superb editing work, to Bela Virag and Alex Petofi for their brilliance in helping me extinguish the daily computer fires, and for my first lessons in artificial intelligence, and to Elizabeth Petofi for so enthusiastically and professionally transcribing all my tapes.

CONTENTS

FEMININE
FUSION

A WORD TO
THE READER

Every small child gracing this planet has, at one time or another, looked around and felt utterly cheated and entrapped in the seemingly unjust constriction of a boy's or girl's body. Casting the eye at the advantages of the other, children quickly learn the game of comparison. How often does the little girl secretly feel her brother to be more beloved and given more attention or value than she? What little boy does not silently envy the tenderness shown by his father to the female members of his family, who are rewarded with sympathy when they are hurt, while he is tersely reminded that "boys don't cry"?

I have written this book to respond to so many people who are struggling to heal the sense that they are not as worthy as another simply because they are the "wrong" gender according to their subconscious imprints from birth or cultural values and limitations imposed on them by virtue of being male or female.

The truth is that we are both male and female! When these two polarity energies *within us* are brought into the most exquisite alignment, they rush together to cause a subsequent fusion that bursts forth into a new energy powerful enough to transform our lives and our world!

The world has become too obsessed with external, material reality to remember that the subtle nuances of energy flows offer the crucial guiding light that directs our lives into channels of fulfillment and purpose. Thus far we have been shaped by a world chartered through masculine energy, the energy of form and volition. There is another kind of energy that is invisible to the eye but is the very source material of all potential. This is the feminine energy, divine spiritual consciousness that expresses itself through formless essence rather than structured matter.

We must now look deeper than just the reality of form (the masculine energy) in order to find ourselves anew. Our educational, social, and planetary systems have become too sluggish and stagnant to propel us onto the next evolutionary plateau. We need desperately to quicken our understanding of the laws of energy so that we can penetrate the seemingly insurmountable problems we face and bask in the peace of solutions. These unknowns are likely to defy all our technological prowess because they have been placed squarely in the path by our very souls in order to awaken an octave of reality more complex than just the plains of matter. In short, the next evolutionary ladder is quite uncompromisingly that of the spirit! And this is the feminine energy.

The way of the masculine or *yang* energy simply cannot take us up to these new levels of existence because the natural flow of the masculine moves outward to structure, not inward to "knowing," as does the feminine. We simply cannot continue our external expansion any further until we begin to learn about these inner realms of existence. The hunger for power and control have reached the point of critical mass, precipitating destruction. We must begin to explore the whys and the meanings that gift us the recognition of the hologram. Holographic perception allows us to recognize how all that is converges and interweaves through the balance of cause and effect, which is called *karma*. We must learn to see all the way around the circle, or the hologram, to actually comprehend truth.

Happily, this is a great and rewarding adventure that will add a new dimension to our human experience. The way of the feminine is gentle but powerful, extensive but inclusive. When

I speak of the feminine, I am not referring to the outer expression of females, I am using the word to describe the energy force that pertains to the spiritual world of essence, the inner dimensions of perception and knowing. Throughout this book I will use the words *feminine, female,* or *yin* to describe a category of energy especially related to the direction of its flow. It is the metaphor of energy flowing back to its source. Feminine energies describe very inward faculties such as intuition, empathy, encompassing, spirituality. Masculine, or yang, energies are those forces that extend outward, such as manifesting, rational, linear, protecting. Thus, yang energy moves out to form manifestation, and yin energy circles more inward to essence.

The feminine energy is possessed not only by women, but by all of us, and can be easily awakened through the intention of our consciousness. Too many men have suffered from disconnection with their inner, divine knowing because they have been taught that intuition and related talents are "sissy stuff" or just useless quirks of nature. I hope you will find it as fascinating as I do to become aware of the feminine energies that pervade all levels of life for both men and women. The contemplation of what we can do with these magnificent feminine energies will consume our creative capacities in the future as we learn to use these skills of human potential on all levels of life. In fact, the future depends on our capacity to find more comprehensive and inclusive ways of living through the mastery of these feminine source energies that help us to relate to life in a new way.

This is not a feminist book. It is not an either/or evaluation of masculine versus feminine. The Western mind sometimes becomes confused when it encounters something that does not follow the illusion that things that are different are in polarity or that opposites ultimately are joined. Rather, the interface between the masculine and the feminine is more like the yin and the yang, which are described not as disconnected polarities, but as energies that flow into each other.

Unlike the last few thousand years, in which women were excluded from male domination, men in the new feminine era

will not be excluded, but rather included. The male body can
support the feminine psyche with pleasure and joy and can express
these energies in ways that will truly alter the future. As we each
explore the inner male and female, we will inevitably and consciously come to the fusion of the two!

With great love,
Chris

THE GREAT
INHERITANCE

Feminine energy is the new bright star on the horizon of consciousness! It has shone silently in the heavens, awaiting the point in human evolution from which we could look up above the horizon of our daily existence and wonder who we are and what we are about. Seized with a despair so deep that we cannot even fathom its source or outcome, we must at long last begin a new journey that may seem to seek the stars but actually seeks to reach the self. We need desperately to discover meaning and purpose in our lives and our world so that we can return from the living dead and regain our strength to live. We have reached the limit, in centuries of externalization of reality, of what life can support in the raging war of polarity, separation, and indifference. We must turn the tide of evolutionary force and bring the flow of consciousness back into the depth of life's mysteries and purpose, which are held within feminine knowing.

The feminine energy is an inherent facet of the whole human. It is an intricate and subtle aspect of our spiritual being inherited by everyone, men and women alike. It is a great inheritance because it is the energy that binds the future and the past. It merges experience and knowing into a present of superb potential. When we are conscious in each moment, we have the capacity to access all knowing, so that questions and answers, problems and solutions, swirl in together to form a reality shaped by our own selves. Feminine energy orchestrates the synergy of our lives by getting us in touch with our soul, from which all purpose and reality stem. We must seek to activate this inheritance, which is our birthright. In accordance with the feminine energy itself, this seeking cannot be accomplished through doing, but only through the discovery of this great inheritance, the feminine energy, as it lives energetically in the life force present in all beings. Now is the moment to become aware that there are laws of energy that govern all manifestations and that we can perceive them and learn to use their guiding influence to restructure even the cycles of life.

Each of us longs for more than we feel is available in the individual body. In the far reaches of our genetic makeup are the memories of our mother's and father's bodies. Beyond these are the historic embodiments of our grandparents. Hidden from the grasp of linear reality are the whispers of our own multi-incarnations, through which we have imprinted myriad impressions of what is male and what is female. These very encodings seem to bind us to a conglomerate of body associations that string together cultural, physical, emotional, and even spiritual percepts in isolated strands of separate or opposite cellular memory of gender. These memories have slept within us long enough.

As each being is irrevocably part and parcel of mother and father, each being also carries within it the inheritance of the feminine. Our genetic inheritance was perfectly designed by nature so that the male and female contribute together to form a new being. This half-and-half genetic design gives everyone both male and female attributes. Perhaps it will shock you to realize that you are indeed both male and female, but the most fantastic adventure begins when you discover what you can do with these energies in your daily life!

There is a woman in everyone, a woman of many dimensions. There is a woman of the physical, who may express feminine energy as physical nurturing, healing, flowing motion, or giving birth. The feminine is also expressed in the mental by seeking merging in all ideas, in creative force; but consciousness is more than an aspect of the body or the mind, it is a spiritual essence inherent in us all. By exploring who we actually are, the feminine energy will be free to express that power individually and collectively. The feminine gifts of fusion and merging have become a mandate at this point of our evolution so that humanity can continue its presence. Only through the gateway of these energies can we hope to secure survival for ourselves and our children's children.

Over the aeons, only a few evolved beings have held mastery over the feminine arts of knowing and intuitive consciousness. Nurtured in protected environments, these great masters and sages from every continent on earth, including such avatars as Jesus the Christ and Buddha, have practiced attuning the living force essences.

You and I must seek to translate what they learned and mastered into a new style of living, being, and experiencing. Through the fusion of natural tendencies, such as knowing and loving, whole realities may occur that bring a quality to life that cannot be coerced into existence via the old ways of control and constrictive management of human relationships, global or local.

The quest for these seemingly elusive energies is not a pastime for the self-infatuated, the self-absorbed narcissistic individual filling up vacant space; it is an urgent necessity for humanity at large, because our entire species is undeniably at the brink of self-destruction. It is an illusion to think that someone else (either a person or a technology) will come along and save us from the very challenges we have set up for ourselves. We have come too far to retreat from the funnel of initiation; it is our turn to press through the threshold and establish a whole new order of existence.

Identification and integration of the feminine energy will cause a natural fusion of the feminine with the masculine to reenact a perfect combination within a plane of existence of a higher nature than that which has been expressed, so far, between men and women. Discovery of the feminine essence in its application will ultimately catapult the whole of humanity onto another level of expression and existence in which the fusion of feminine and masculine forces will create a new adaptive species of humankind. It is the nature of feminine energy to be adaptive, flexible, fluid. That is what is needed. It is within us; let us find it now!

2

FEMININE ALCHEMY

Each of us is a masterpiece of alchemy, a divine blending of elements that interact with each other to catalyze a fertile soup of individual potential. Feminine alchemy is a magical mixture of nuance and gesture, hormones and emotions, energies and actions, that embrace multitudinous styles of female expression on the part of men and women, children, societies, and cultures. As it is true that energy is never stagnant, but constantly changing and in motion, this dynamic alchemy pushes us into continually perceiving and experiencing our own reality in a new way. By studying the feminine alchemy within us, we are able to comprehend the subtleties of our relationship to the outside world. For it is through the lens of feminine consciousness that we are able to view the basic components of relationship as *energy*, whether it is a place or a person.

The world is neither accidental nor ultimately chaotic. It has directions, patterns and pulsations, and the law of cause and effect, or karma, shapes our reality. The more we recognize the energetic elements that compose a structure or a person, the more we can perceive our choice of responding in a certain way to that relationship or to that environment. In short, each individual is the alchemist who mixes and stirs his or her own pot.

We can explore how innate feminine energies move within

our emotional bodies, our physical, mental, and spiritual bodies. We can also observe their reflection in our daily lives, as they are interpreted within our particular culture, within the family that we have chosen, in nature, in styles, as they are reflected in the world around us.

Once we identify feminine presence, we are able to see its effect on everything and everyone around us. Nothing in life stands alone, but all energies are a magnificent mix that create some perfect, unique reality. As we are able to observe that mixing, that feminine alchemy, we understand on a more profound energetic level why it is that we respond so uniquely to places and people, based on that interaction of the feminine energy as it comes into contact with the world.

Feminine awareness is the precipice of power. With it we can leap off the edge of passivity into the magnificent, swirling energies of the creative force that transform us from the inert observers of life into the masters of form.

THE BODY

The body is the most evident and easily identifiable representation of feminine alchemy expressed in form. Though our bodies are either male or female, the combinations of masculine and feminine energies within each of us are expressed in multitudinous variations of body type and tendency. It is fascinating to perceive, even in the newborn baby, the most basic components of each as they are uniquely combined from the beginning.

For example, a male baby may demonstrate a sensitivity, a passivity, an expression, or an attitude that is very feminine. A small girl baby may be very active and express her will through her body, exemplary of masculine force. These early patternings do continue and amplify themselves as the child grows. That quiet and passive little boy infant may become a sensitive five-year-old who likes to draw and to paint and is very careful in using his body to touch plants or animals; the very active girl baby may become the proverbial tomboy who wants to climb and swing and jockey for center position as king of the mountain. These two children will seek out models of behavior that confirm and increase their capacity to express the basic mixtures of energy within them. Physically as well, the body will develop in ways that amplify the inner tendencies, building itself upon the energies that it is given from the moment of conception. Thus one child may develop highly acute sensory capacities, while another may be motor-oriented. The body will also build a metabolic response mechanism that allows it to carry out the type of action required by the prevailing energy.

Puberty is the great changeover from a stage in which both the male and the female energies were expressed, to a time when the energies are more crystallized and are centered in either the male or female body. At puberty the hormones that begin to sculpt the body into its final identity come into play. Many parents experience alarm when their darling son suddenly begins to express himself aggressively.

I will never forget the day at thirteen when I suddenly awoke as if from a trance to realize that I was indeed a girl. I had taken great pride in the fact that as a quarterback on my neighborhood football team, the only girl, I was the fastest runner. I was carrying the ball when two boys tackled me to the ground. They cheered at recovering the ball, but I was suddenly furious. Not only did it hurt my newly emerging female body, but I felt the aggressive intent as a personal attack, and my feelings were sorely injured! I walked away from the playing field, my identity as a tomboy shattered, to enter the inevitable world of the female.

The stimulation of hormones that brings us through puberty very much expresses feminine alchemy. At different times in our lives, the hormonal levels alter to such a degree that they can actually influence our predisposition to masculine or feminine expression. A man whose testosterone levels are low will tend to be much more mellow than one whose male hormones are literally driving him to release that thrusting yang energy. Likewise, the woman whose hormonal levels show a higher mixture of male hormones will posture within the more driving force of male expression.

The endocrine system is the secret designer of who we are and how we convey ourselves to the outside world in terms of our pervasive masculine or feminine energy. In the future we will learn to use the technology of consciousness to balance the masculine and feminine essences released by the endocrine system in such a way as to dissolve the aging process and influence even the shape and texture of our bodies. As we begin to understand how the subtle energies of the master endocrine glands, the pineal and the pituitary, extend beyond the spiral of matter into the unmanifest octaves of spiritual essence, we will realize how the soul itself is a partner to the influences of culture, family, and genetics in sculpting the human psyche.

There are many interesting quirks in the body's expression of feminine energy: witness the great big man who looks so overpowering and yet turns out to be the proverbial teddy bear with the soft, soft heart. The soft-tissued body, the rounded face, the placement of fat stores, the pitch of the voice, even the shape of the fingers cue us as to the alchemic mixes of the feminine.

The body in motion provides one of the greatest expressions of the feminine. There are nuances and gestures that are indisputably feminine in character, whether made by a man or a woman. These are not the gestures of pretense that are usually thought of as negative, but the fluid, soft motions that express receptivity—the trademark of the feminine. We all recognize the grace of feminine movement, and when we allow ourselves to move in those ways we feel the gentle, loving currents of energy that enhance our feeling of well-being.

By practicing gentleness with your body movements you can actually shift the yin/yang (feminine/masculine) balance of your being. If you are moving with soft gesture, your countenance will follow your physical motion. The reverse is true as well. If you want to be more assertive, try strong, swift motions and you will feel yourself extending outward as the yang energy pumps through the muscles and meridians of the body.

Try this exercise.

Stand up and close your eyes, so that your Emotional Body is not afraid of appearing foolish, and begin to move around the room in a gliding fashion. Stretch out as if you were embracing the air. Now, standing still, open your arms to the sides and bring them over your head, touching the fingertips like a dancer. Then bring them down gracefully and up again several times. Now stand with the left foot forward and slowly swing your arms alternately backward over your head like a windmill. Keep doing this, becoming more lateral in your movements until your arms are crossing in front of your face.

This is an excellent exercise for executives because it opens the shoulders, where the body holds its thoughts and feelings about responsibility. By altering the direction of force to a sweeping, circular gesture of openness, you are practicing inclusive messages that invite sharing, cooperation, and mutual problem-solving—the only choice for the future.

STYLES

Clothing styles are a direct expression of feminine alchemy. The capacity to use clothes to combine and balance the male/female energy, or to express that essence energy by making it visible, is a way of cueing the outside world about what we feel inside. Women and men have always used clothing to express, perhaps unconsciously, their own attunement to their male or female orientation.

In today's modern world, women often dress in a masculine form because they are expressing attributes of the male to which they aspire: decisiveness, power, authority, and control. What could be more controlling than a suit that holds the range of motion of the body basically to the forward projection of the arms? You cannot even lift up the arms, which is the best direction of inspiration and growth.

On the other side are women who dress seductively in order to enhance the awareness of their feminine energy, because their consciousness is so intimately intertwined with their sense of femininity in its sexual application. Often it is the woman who has learned from her family that she must appear sexy, who is the most insecure about those very attributes and so focuses attention on her body in an attempt to be recognized. The pain of not being accepted may be so great that she actually is very aggressive or angry and closed down in the heart—the antithesis of the feminine. She may choose flashy styles and colors, such as red, to call attention to herself.

In fact, colors are wonderful messengers of masculine or feminine allegiance. The yang colors of red and orange seek visibility, and the browns, grays, and mixtures of black portray solidarity, sobriety, and authority. The softer colors that blend or are more muted express the feminine passive, less defined, and more surrendering attitudes.

Men also use colors to state their sense of self. As the male begins to hunger for the female within, he may explore the sensibilities of feminine colors, the soft pinks and pastels that bespeak the more tender energy inside him.

I remember as a child feeling great rebelliousness at being forced to wear pink while my elder sister was given the blue colors. I recognize now how much I needed, from the perspective of my soul's incarnational lessons, to experience love, to learn to radiate love, and pink is the color of love. Being born a premature baby, I spent six weeks in an incubator. I think premature babies are instilled with a sense of being expelled or cast out from the womb without making a choice, so they often imprint a reaction of denial. I certainly came into this life with the imprint of denial about choosing to be born, and that initial love bonding did not take place because there was no one to hold me. Pink was exactly the color I needed to fill the hole of separation, yet it was the color that I most rejected and resisted because, unconsciously, I was already invested in that denial. What we resist so often is the key to the lessons that are necessary for our soul's growth. Even in something as simple as the styles we wear and the colors we choose, we are able to see exactly how that feminine energy within us is being accepted or acknowledged and which octaves of expression are open to us.

PARENTS

Our initial and most primary teaching about feminine energy comes from our parents—from the alchemy of feminine energy present within both father and mother, and also in terms of the alchemic reactions as the two of them relate to each other. The small child watches and emulates the postures and pretenses staged by the parents individually and as they demonstrate the attributes of each in relationship. "You are a boy" or "Girls do this" is spoken over and over again to teach children right from the beginning what it means to belong to the club of gender. The father and the mother will reinforce the patterns and attitudes they acknowledge within each other about what is acceptable and appropriate expression of male and female energies and then transfer these patterns and attitudes to the child.

When we prepare to come into this life, we very carefully choose our parents, each one, selecting souls with a certain feminine alchemy that either mirrors what we lack and need to learn or what we have and need to outgrow. As we take on these imprints from our parents, we begin to process and assimilate the energies that relate to our alchemical mix. All of this blinding realization goes on, of course, *after* we have grown up enough to consciously contemplate our fate as men and women, *after* we have absorbed tons of stifling imprints as to how we should be and what we should do in the world.

It is thrilling to be aware of ourselves as the product of our parents from the perspective of feminine alchemy. Through identifying the feminine balances within *them*, we begin to see a clear mirror of our own repertoire. As we become conversant with feminine energy, we can observe elements in our parents that we apply or model or disregard as we ourselves grow and learn to handle the male and female energies. By recognizing the primordial and yet divine energetics of feminine energy, we understand completely how it is that they are our teachers, reflecting to us combinations of energy that unveil even the most secretive aspects of the self.

One of the most obvious things they reflect is the balance between the negative and the positive feminine energies. The positive feminine is nurturing, loving, perceiving, receiving, and knowing, and the negative feminine misuses all these energies. The negative represents the cattiness and the critical aspect of the feminine personality, the tendency to gossip, to belittle, to destroy, or to manipulate by negating the power or energy of another or by using knowing, nurturing, and especially sexuality to create dependence, control, and dominance. Many mothers and wives use this negative feminine method of creating dependence in relationship to express the self. They may use nurturing, cooking, or making love as a weapon to cajole someone, whether a child or a husband, to do their bidding. This is a blatant misuse of feminine energy.

The negative feminine continually levies the Emotional Body to maintain or maneuver reality. Using fear tactics is a classical negative feminine technique. Men and women who possess the natural psychic, intuitive talents of the feminine tend to manipulate partners, children, and colleagues by influencing them with negative prognoses or prophesying negative events and dire potentials, rather than pursuing problem-solving through positive channels. The negative feminine knows the secrets of probable reality and, like the soothsayers of old, uses the art of subtle persuasion to direct the flow.

This negative engineering of reality comes from the emotional comfort of being the power behind the throne, of being the one who can have an influence without being visible, without taking responsibility, all the while maneuvering these energies in play in such a way as to create what is desired. This desire usually comes from negative emotions such as revenge, envy, and competition. It thrives on negative relationship, on projection and utter dependence on the rival, who takes up all the emotional space.

Manipulation of power in these subtle arenas is very seductive, and seduction itself is one of the most negative attributes of the negative feminine. To deploy the emotional body for psychological warfare is standard practice, and very often the target doesn't even know the truth because the hunger to be chosen or engaged is such an overriding emotion.

We learn these techniques from the game of survival taught in the home. Both mother and father may exhibit complex mixtures of the negative feminine. Certainly both parents portray stereotypical roles that only thinly veil the emotional male/female tendencies they learned from their parents. As we seek to know the nuances that express their emotional makeup, we can begin truly to recognize our parents and ourselves.

We may select a father whose feminine energy is very strong and positive in order to learn that we can communicate and come into relationship with feminine energy as it lives within the male. This is a great blessing for a sensitive little boy who is thus spared so much embarrassment and confusion when the world refuses to offer any support for those energies. A female whose father has this feminine energy can learn about finer avenues of feminine communication with the opposite sex, and this will most definitely influence the type of mate she will choose for herself.

If the feminine energy is strong in us, and we are aware of it and have mastered it to some degree, we do not need to have that energy projected outside ourselves. As we free our mothers from the confines of a narrowly defined female role, we may witness an expansion of their feminine composition to one that contains more yang, or masculine force, than feminine. This is a common occurrence in today's world, as women are becoming more visible in the expression of their masculine energy. Since they express more of the masculine, their partners have the luxury and the opportunity to begin to express more of their feminine energy. Whereas the stereotype of male and female was simple and clearly marked fifty years ago, these energies in today's world are a product of an evolutionary alchemy that is shaping a whole new potential of human relationship.

CULTURES

Cultures, too, express a predominant and individualized adaptation of feminine energy. Some cultures use the feminine as an intricate part of family patterning or as a component of cultural expression so that the art, the music, and the value structure of the culture is geared to the expression of the feminine. This is much more evident in Eastern cultures than in Western cultures, which tend to be more oriented toward the masculine.

Earlier peoples, who recognized or were formed and based upon the mysteries of life and death, mysteries of the gods, were more in tune with nature and expressed a high understanding of feminine energy. Feminine alchemy was thematically expressed in coherent and articulate descriptions of life. In many of these cultures, the mother was an expression of the divine. The mystery of giving birth, the mystery of bringing forth life itself, was considered part of the expression of God. There were many goddesses who lent their power to the creative recognition of these mysteries.

Scores of great classical artists used the feminine principle as the basis for their work. The bodies in their paintings were voluptuous and feminine and expressed the nurturing, flowing, and giving energies of the feminine. Often their statues, drawings, and fetishes included graphic depictions of the female anatomy expressing the power of fertility. Their music expressed the passion and the mysterious elements of the emotional body that have always been considered part of the feminine domain.

Much great poetry and literature expresses a hunger for relationship to the spiritual, feminine element of life. To write about seeking the source of life's purpose is an attempt to communicate, to touch, and to give form to the feminine energy from a universal octave.

PLACE OF BIRTH

Viewing our place of birth from the perspective of feminine alchemy is a fascinating echo of the degree to which we felt welcomed when we came into body. The Emotional Body associates our birthplace with the degree of nurturing, protecting, loving energies we experienced at birth.

At the Light Institute, we work with balancing our energies as they relate to the place we were born, as if our birthing place were an actual person or living entity. If we are able to feel that it was a nurturing place for us, welcoming us to this planet, to this earth, we begin to feel full and can imprint our Emotional Body with the sense of being accepted, desired, and a part of something.

One of the most elementary aspects of feeling worthy in life is being in touch with the need to be a part of some place, someone. When you experience that your birthplace was a magical and sacred spot on this living earth, you will feel a natural opening of the heart that is very healing. It matters not that it was a nondescript hospital or an overcrowded city. It was a choice of the all-knowing Higher Self, gifting that place with the indestructible purity of life itself.

Contemplate for a moment your own feelings about the place in which you were born. If you long to feel connected in your life, go back and reconnect spiritually with your birthplace. Both mother and child usually feel something special about this birthplace because emotionally our trust in the nurturing feminine energy is intertwined with those birthing feelings.

Someone else who comes to our birthplace might find it foreboding, even dangerous. Yet we may notice only the greenery, the plants, and the beauty of the area. The childlike ability to experience that beauty comes precisely from our connection with the feminine energy. Often the soul selects a place of birth to more finely hone the feminine energy by setting us in a seemingly masculine or difficult environment, which forces us to find a solution to the problem of the coexistence of these two forces.

FEMALE ENERGY IN NATURE

Mother Nature herself is an exquisite example of feminine alchemy, orchestration of life in energetic balance. Being in a natural environment offers a magnificent opportunity to practice the feminine energy, because to perceive the laws of nature we must be able to tune in to those exquisite levels that shape the invisible order of the world. By using our psychic capacity, for example, we can attune our vibrations to the negative ions in the atmosphere that are so healing to our physical bodies.

By perceiving the life force energy that radiates from plants, we can experience the incredible balance of life it represents— the plant breathes out oxygen, which we breathe in; we breathe out carbon dioxide, which the plant breathes in. We must come to acknowledge our interdependent relationships with each other and to experience very directly, very physically, how communing with the feminine through nature nourishes us, increases and enhances our life force and our potential to become more fully conscious.

Communication with nature is an invitation to consciousness. Becoming aware that even rocks emit electrical impulses and are therefore living helps us to tap in to cosmic energies that so powerfully teach us the divine principles of the hologram. Thus we experience that we are an integral part of something larger than ourselves, and that necessitates our spiritual recognition in order to maintain a relationship of balance.

Nature is a magnificent expression of feminine alchemy through the infinite variations of form—that which is lush and inviting and encompassing and that which is sweeping, strong, and extending. Through nature's perfect alchemy, we can sift the energies and pluck for ourselves exactly the expression of nurturing that fits our own expression in each moment and through our lifelong patterns. Each of us may look out at the same scenario and see there the elements that we interrupt as masculine or feminine according to our own emotional association. We take our cues from Mother Nature as we visually intuit the masculine and feminine forces. When we observe a terrain and call it "masculine," we are often describing lines and trajectories or pointed areas that show force. High mountains, for example, have a thrusting energy that has the feel of the yang, whereas rolling hills, valleys, and flowing river areas are perceived as being nurturing and yin. Each of these terrains is echoed by the human form with its masculine straight lines or feminine curves that express the motion and quality of energy inherent in each.

I am always amazed at people's reactions to Galisteo. Some find its vast spaces and barren plains a magnificent expression of masculine form. Others feel absolutely cradled in its wonderful basin and experience the reassuring rocking of the ancient sea, still present two thousand feet below its surface, as the very essence of Mother Earth herself.

Nature is especially suited for the exploration of the feminine because it provides us with such a rich array of sensual experience. The smells, the colors, the shapes, as well as the textures and flavors, provided by Mother Nature allow us to amplify and to enjoy the physical perception of our self and the world.

All of nature carries within it the imprint of every evolution of its many forms, as well as the actual experiences with which all living beings have impregnated the atmosphere. All wars, all deaths, all laughter, all birth, echo and radiate out from the trees, the rocks, from the earth itself, as the organic energies of any place absorb and hold life and record its history. This holding is the way of the feminine.

I remember once having a mystical experience of this recording effect in California. I came upon a magnificent oak tree that had lived for hundreds of years. It stood alone on a hillside, commanding the view in a great visual sweep. Such love and respect swelled up in me as I entered its canopy of branches that I could not resist embracing it.

Hugging its wonderful trunk, I felt like a child holding the thighs of a grandmother. A pleasant feeling came over me as I lingered alone there with the warm sunlight on my back. The slow-moving fluid sap of the tree stirred a psychic resonance within me. Without consciously choosing to do so, I entered the sap. As I felt the movement of the sap, it was as if I were looking across the cambrian layers that recorded each year's growth and perceptions. The sap seemed to be the medium of memory for the tree. Somehow I became the eyes of the sap that was holding the images the oak tree had seen over the hundreds of years it had existed.

Initially, I saw the red plaid jacket of some outdoorsman as if I were seeing the image through the rather sticky, opaque lens of the sap. I then saw a hawk moving in slow motion, almost suspended in the sky. I saw each as if it were composed of trillions of pinpricks of light. It seemed as though the light held together the form, and perhaps, in some magical way, as the oak tree took in light for the purpose of photosynthesis, the composition of images entered intact, with that streaming of light.

I then saw a series of beings, Native Americans, who approached the tree. They seemed to be of several centuries. Some were dressed in different styles of clothing with different patternings and markings. Some came to gather the acorns, some to rest, but all of them acknowledged the tree with respect.

Tears streamed down my face as I witnessed this expanse of life. I felt an instant perception of the difference in density and salinity between my tears and the sap, as my tears brought me back from the inner reaches of the slowly moving energy within the tree.

Several days later I walked again through the hills with three other women. We passed this beautiful oak tree and moved down the hill into an area that was known to be used by the Native American women as a place of sacred menstruation. Many groups around the world have recognized that menstruation is a very powerful "medicine" of the female. Most traditional cultures treat it as a sacred monthly occurrence that necessitates either particular rituals or some socially coherent act separating it from daily life. This area was on the edge of a grove of trees surrounding a small meadow. Here stood another of these magnificent oak trees. Definitely feminine in energy, she seemed to me to be the Mother of All Oaks, spreading her branches over a massive area of the field. She had grown up next to a large, flat boulder. Here, my friends told me, the Native American women would gather and spend their days of menstruation together, encamped in this small meadow. There was a tiny spring of water that emerged from the ground near this oak tree and produced lush grasses, watercress, and wild flowers.

As we stopped to rest on the rock, I mused to myself that we were, the four of us, a likely composition of so many women who must have gathered there: two of us nearing the end of our menstrual cycles, one in full flower of female productivity and procreative potential, and Alexandra, our beautiful young one, fresh on the path of womanhood.

Joanna suggested that we meditate and take in the energy of this wonderful place. Sitting there, I fell into that delicious empty state that has nurtured my knowing throughout my life. My psychic awareness became immediately attuned to the imprints being held over the entire area: by the rock, the earth, the oak tree, and the meadow. I began to perceive the infrared imprints of women who had once gathered by the tree, just as we were now.

As I began to tune to the astral energy, I was able to perceive the women who were relaxing under the tree and around its edges. They were giggling and teasing each other. It was a most amazing experience, for I know that I actually heard the communications as sound. Though they were, of course, speaking in their language, I understood as if they were speaking in my language. I remember the particular high trilling sound of a young girl's voice. This was her first experience by the menstruation tree, and she was exhilarated yet a little fearful. Another girl, slightly older than she, was being teased by two other girls about her flirtations with a young man.

I remember that it seemed so natural to me because the conversation could have taken place in any culture at any time, and I smiled to myself about the possibility that there are, indeed, universal themes that have been carried on within the human family from the dawn of community. The thrill and excitement of becoming a woman, available for the attentions of a partner or mate, are, and always will be, a part of the human scenario. Their laughter will remain with me always, and as I related what I had experienced to Joanna, Alexandra, and Elisabeth, we smiled at each other in recognition of that universal female pastime, to plot and tease and absorb ourselves with the adventure of attracting a mate.

By becoming aware of feminine alchemy as it expresses itself throughout our life, we can understand the gifts that are given to us through the experience of living and how it is that so many of our emotional perspectives of whether we are loved enough, acknowledged enough, abundant enough, come simply from the balance or imbalance of feminine energies. For men and women equally, the feminine energies around us open the threshold to a supercharged reality in which the self resides.

Think about these things when you are creating your physical surroundings: as you are choosing your clothes, your furniture, your style of self-expression. Look at the lines, the colors, and the textures, and feel whether or not you have created a balance of the feminine/masculine energy in your environment or whether it is imbalanced on one side or the other. Of course, that balance is specific to you and your energies, but it is illuminating to view the self from this perspective of representative surroundings.

If, wherever you are each day, you would simply attune to these feminine energies as they are present in the environment around you, you will be able to enhance your own experience of the feminine. Even in an apartment in a large city, the one plant or animal or rock you might have will give you nourishment and communicate with you on those internal, feminine wavelengths that extend your consciousness into the stream of life.

3

MASKS OF GENDER

Socially, we live behind masks of gender that make it easy for us to relate to each other through our immediate recognition of specific roles we've designated for the purpose of social communication. Every society has a rule book of behavior considered appropriate for males and females. These behavior codes become the masks that homogenize developing personalities at initial stages of childhood and direct our development as individuals into predictable categories that make us recognizable to the society in which we grow up. Of course, the most simple category is male or female, and thus we are labeled early by our gender. This is extremely painful to many of us because we may feel that this exterior "packaging" precludes us from feelings we want to share or even things we would love to do. Those around us base the content of their communication with us on whether we are male or female. This becomes a point of reference that is layered over our primary self and begins to define who we are. In short, it is a mask that satisfies the outside world in terms of our place within the group.

We are taught to use these masks of gender to identify ourselves and to help us fit into a groove that makes us acceptable to others and to ourselves. Of course, from culture to culture, what is considered to be male or female posture can vary incredibly, simply because each group has developed a code of communication that facilitates living in its unique environment. What makes it work is not so much the definition of male or female behavior itself as the culture's collective agreement to conform to whatever behavior is set forth.

It is interesting to note that in many cultures, although the female is not officially acknowledged or given equal value, behind the scenes, within the household, she reigns supreme. I have witnessed this many times in the Americas, where the social emphasis seems to be on the macho male, but behind the scenes it is the woman who makes decisions, who handles the money, and who directs the life of the family. Because of the actual power the woman wields in private, she is willing to pretend otherwise in public. One of the most frightening predicaments for women in any culture occurs when they become conscious of being more powerful than the man, who is supposed to protect and take care of them. Women from around the world have reported this dilemma to me with great sorrow and confusion.

Part of this energy predicament stems from the cultural insistence that males be so visible externally. In this kind of cultural role playing, little boys experience a great deal of insecurity about the difference between pretending power and actual power. From a very early age, their mothers teach them to pretend to be the boss. Of course they are utterly dependent upon the willingness of the mother to pretend the play. This may be an important clue as to why mothers are put on pedestals and continue to be of absolute importance to men in those cultures that value— almost worship—their mothers but ignore their wives!

On the other hand, since the female identity in all cultures is fluid and has been trained to yield, a woman does not lose her sense of self when the situation calls for surrender. Even while acquiescing, she may actually feel more secure than the man because she is accustomed to bending. She recognizes that there is a game in play. The male is often unaware that it is a game and believes he is in charge.

Even though the exterior presentation or mask of the female

may be much more nebulous than that of the male, the woman has learned to measure her presence by the feelings that are in motion. She knows how to interpret the world through the recognition of subtle energies and therefore feels much safer with chaos and constant flux of feelings. She can attune to the angers, fears, and hopes behind the masks of those around her and therefore is able to identify and interpret what is really happening and which way things will go. This intuitive approach is a much more dependable system of measuring reality because it allows the female to comprehend the source energies that influence the actions of others. It is much easier to be invisible, "the power behind the throne" that directs the course of events without being judged on the result. The mask of the wife hiding behind the status of the husband is a good example of this. She can persuade or influence others without risking the kind of exposure that might change the world's opinion of her and therefore cause her to experience anxiety about herself.

In the Western world, as survival becomes less a matter of physical, and more a matter of subtle skills, the male and the female must become more homogeneous, even androgynous. The old divisions of the male out in the world and the female in the home are hardly even applicable to today's reality. The demands for successful societal living are simply too stringent for such simplicity.

Today, society places great value on the "doing" of life. The conversational patter of "What do you do?" has caused so much discomfort to housewives that they have rushed into the marketplace to find an answer that has reshaped family life and thrown males and females into a new dance of polarity that has not yet reached its frenzied peak. In time, the pendulum will swing back into a more expanded scenario that will include attributes of wisdom, caring, sharing, healing, and loving as valuable assets to be communicated or emulated, rather than stultifying postures, attitudes, and behaviors of isolated gender.

Though we love to pretend and tease each other about what it is to be a "real male" or a "real female," there is a lot of confusion about who we actually are. The greater this confusion, the more dependent we are on stereotypical codes of behavior, dress, and styles of life that make it as easy as possible to identify what is expected of us and how to live comfortably in the world. Thus we find ourselves clutching these masks of gender in a futile attempt to avoid the challenge of self-discovery or the fear of "falling out of bounds"!

The more recognition you have of energies in you that belong to the opposite gender, the greater may be your confusion, until you release your fear of the implications of these energies and actually put them to use. It is often scary to feel that inside is lurking energy that you think belongs to the opposite sex. Given a multidimensional format that allows you to see yourself from the perspective of a soul that has experienced many lifetimes in both male and female bodies, you can begin to acknowledge this energy not as some body mix-up, but as an important part of your repertoire. Opting to view yourself in this new light can bring you great pleasure and even be a tremendous help in your life.

It is important to explore your own individual mask of gender, how you use it, and what your underlying attitudes are about the restrictions placed upon you because of it. Your soul has chosen your body for this lifetime to facilitate certain lessons that are easier to learn from this particular body. Since certain recognized traits are acknowledged almost universally in relationship to the male and female energy, it is important to ask yourself if you are hiding behind these traits or are using them in a creative way in your life. Does a stereotypical man, who is expected to be strong, unemotional, and rational, hide his tenderness, his longings, and his fear of his own vulnerability behind the mask of profession-alism or masculine posture? And does the woman, who is ex-pected to succumb or surrender, use seduction or the pretense of not understanding to hide her determination and her will to secretly manipulate the world?

Examine how you have been using the game of male/female "positionality." Not only will you find great amusement in the gesturing and pretending of your role, but by acknowledging your performance, you can let go of the limitation of the role and truly expand your repertoire. Begin by observing the difference in the quality and style of your communication between someone of the same sex and someone of the opposite sex. You can be sure that there is a difference. Even little children discover that men and women are playing opposing roles and that there is an ongoing duel for power and dominance between them. This experience of opposing polarities gives children the message that it is necessary to fight for survival, and we carry on this message through adult life. We use this opposite polarity effect as a sounding board, a reality from which we can bounce back and experience ourselves.

As we are taught to follow in the footsteps of our parents, to emulate the role of the parent of the same sex, we simultaneously learn to project certain characteristics onto the opposite parent because that's what the parent we are emulating does. As we grow up, we simply continue the patterns of relationship we witnessed as children, as if there were no other choices. The tragedy is that unless they have some degree of sensitivity and awareness, men and women are often so consumed with using each other as sounding boards, they never learn actually to know each other. They simply mirror and project those qualities they have been taught are appropriate or expected and, therefore, must be reacted to from the opposite polarity.

Because the child is so early imprinted with the nature of polarity relationship as being something that is tenuous and risky, he learns to protect himself by emulating the safe responses used by his own particular gender. It is absolutely crucial to understand this perspective because it speaks of the very essence, the very nature, of male/female relationships.

If your mother and father—consciously or unconsciously—through their behavior, through their very subtle, psychic communication, demonstrated that the male/female relationship was, indeed, an unending duel, that will become the framework into which you will place any person of the opposite gender—thereby

MASKS OF GENDER • 43

drastically constricting and diminishing the quality and potential of your relationships.

If in your primary relationships you learn that the opposite gender is unsafe, you will never be able to express your unique individual talents in the presence of that polarity. The emotional body places too high a priority on safety to allow that risk. You will simply be unable to see that beyond the mask, the physical body, the style of clothing, the posture of the polarity, is someone with an amplitude of expression just like your own.

Expressing male or female energies through stereotypical behavior exposes our innate fear of going into deep experiences. Fear blocks us from growth, from exploration of deep levels of awareness. This is the source of inertia; when self-expression is based on safety, it becomes characterized by habit. We become habitual in our expression, and as we grow older in life, the confines of our male/female expression become narrower. It funnels in, becoming more defensive and more judgmental. Habitual behavior is always characterized by inertia and superficiality because it requires so little presence in the moment.

In order to become conscious of these patterns of projection, you must be able to see them in action. If you were to stop and ask yourself what you wanted or needed in a partner or a person of the opposite sex, you would begin to see your unconscious repertoire of projections come to the surface. Try listing those things for yourself. For example, "I need a man to support me, protect me, and guide me. I see him as _____." Or, "I need a woman to nourish me, take care of me, acknowledge me. I see her as _____." All the attributes or faults you list are ones that the other person is mirroring for you. As you become aware of these needs, desires, or attributes, you will see that you are actually projecting onto the other person those qualities that you are not aware of having yourself. You can dissolve this projection as you discover that all those qualities, good and bad, that you see and desire from someone outside you, are actually already inside you in the form of energies that magnetize "like" energies in others.

It is important to explore these particulars of projection, because as long as you view them in the domain of polarity, you will be unable to acknowledge them as aspects of yourself that are available to you. Unencumbered by projection, you can discover a unique being, not a stereotype, not someone you measure against a preconceived image of the opposite polarity or with whom you must struggle to survive or commune.

It is easy, through the mask of gender, to convey to the world that one wishes to be viewed in a particular manner, whether that is as a macho male or a vulnerable female. Those expressions are easy and can be done even by such superficial avenues as dress and style. However, to explore the *essence* of the male or the female and to express these essence energies, we must allow them to be living and vital within us so that they are virtually radiating out of our presence. Awakening to recognize these energies takes profound soul-searching. Once we can identify them, the male-female essences are available to us in myriad expressions that can mingle in unique ways to meet any particular experience or situation.

For example, to express the male essence at one moment might be to be mental, or to create structures in the external world, but those structures may simultaneously express the nurturing, protecting masculine energies as well.

Expression of the female, feminine elements at their essence level allows us a wide range of behavior or contribution that the superficial and stereotypical female does not offer us. If we are behaving as the little girl, we have no access to our psychic power or our great capacities to console or to counsel. If we are the feminine martyr being used by the outside world, there is no strength in our invisibility, which so innately characterizes the feminine essence.

The Emotional Body struggles continually to defend its singular image of male or female and ultimately succumbs to that dry, deserted scenario in which only one of them prevails. True qualities that are the essence of male or female must be delineated, each in its own hologram of related expression, and then fused together so that there is a unique balance of male and female. We can integrate the feminine energy with the masculine energy to manifest something new. The feminine lends its propensity to assist by using its wisdom for counseling and its talent for creative vision in concert with the masculine energies of structure and the overt power of form. We cannot hope to become the master of the feminine and to integrate it so as to change our earthly experience without embarking on a path of discovery wherein that which is masculine or that which is feminine takes on an entirely new meaning of expression in our lives. It is only when we take off the masks of gender that we, in effect, come into contact with the essence of male and female energies. Then we are able to experience their complementary nature rather than their polarity; how each amplifies the other. By using the deep currents of yin expression, men and women can learn to apply feminine principles such as orchestration and harmonics to bring fulfillment to their lives.

As the world becomes smaller, we are beginning to outgrow these masks of gender because they simply do not allow us enough amplitude of expression to keep pace with our growing. Inner growth is becoming recognized around the world as absolutely crucial to success in life, to success in relationship, and to joy and happiness on all levels.

4

CHANNELS
OF RELATIONS

One of the most fascinating explorations of the human psyche comes when we delve into the mechanisms of relationship. Myriad patternings are set in motion to teach the child about relationship according to the familial, social, and cultural mandates into which the child is born. Parents teach their child how to identify others and how to express relationship with them. These patterns become "channels of relations" that are instrumental in forming the child's personality and sense of identity or belonging to the world around him. Almost immediately, a new baby is introduced to the accepted channels of relation employed by its family that are superimposed upon any innate or natural energies that were a part of his essential makeup.

However, the essence of our true nature is always there, and any in-depth study of the self must include the recognition that beyond the dance of relationship we do with others is the dance we do with the inner facets of ourselves. Since we all have masculine and feminine attributes, if we can discover how they are interacting, we can enter into a most profound realization of why we relate the way we do with others and their respective inner energies.

Unfortunately, these early interactions always exert a strong pull into the outside world, not the inner world, and eventually they almost completely camouflage the essence energies with which we are born. If you are a boy, you were influenced by the encouragement of all those around you to respond and behave in the manner that identifies you as a boy. The same is true of the girl who from the first moment is treated in ways that teach her how to be a girl.

By the time we reach adulthood, we have learned to cue others as to the type of relationship we are having at any moment with them. We use our voice, our body, and an infinite variety of nuances to let them know if we are available as sexual partners or buddies, bosses or friends. We place others in specific stereotyped categories that help us to be comfortable and even habitual in our interaction with them. Our entire range of emotional, psychic, mental, and spiritual repertoire is easily formulated into an appropriate interchange with anyone we meet. These are channels of relations that we learn early to identify, and we maintain our communications with others in strict accordance with these channels for most of our life.

As with radio or TV channels, we learn to select the one that fits the person with whom we are communicating. We begin with simple, main channels that define our early reality: mommy, daddy, sister, friend, grandparent, busman, policeman, neighbor. We learn to identify and relate to these people by the association of their title, our parents' responses to them, and the way they feel to us. We quickly realize that there is a difference between policeman and neighbor. We learn about physical and social distances that communicate safety both to ourselves and others. We give emotional and even physical closeness as favors of friendship only to certain people. The person at the store is given a certain range of response or level of communication that is different from the one we give to someone who is closer within our field. We computerize all this information about distance, touch, gesture, and expression and incorporate it into the appropriate boxes or channels of relations.

We learn early from our parents to perceive people through these stereotyped descriptions. We observe how our parents act and feel toward them. We know who is approved of by our parents and who is not. We learn that the amount of energy that should be given to anyone in any particular box is dependent upon whether that person is considered close to us or important to our survival or whether he is extraneous to our daily lives, to our success, to our own position in the world.

Relationship is a major theme on this planet today. In order for us to be successful in our attempts to touch each other, we must become aware not only of these channels, but also of the choices we have to make on energetic levels that establish the differences in essence between cultural or genetic boundaries. For example, as we move through the patterns we have accrued, we can teach our consciousness to embrace the true energies of a person, rather than simply the posturing or posing that comes about through social or familial imprinting. The fact that we are of both male and female essence extends the horizon tremendously in terms of our expression. This is further amplified when we place ourselves in relationship to others so that our inner energies can align with theirs. Because of the karma we have had with any given person, we may relate through the face of the male or from the opposite female position. The trick to transformation is achieving a level of consciousness that allows us to identify how and why we are doing this. We may discover, "With this person I am always very aggressive and assertive, but with that person I am always the catty female." As we come to know the energies of each and how they pair up with others, we can scan the dial to find the best connection. Then the person who is playing opposite us must also transform because our connection dissipates on the karmic level, and we no longer fit together in the same old way. Thus, people either exit from our lives or alter the channels of relations to communicate from new levels.

THE FAMILY CHANNEL

Members of other countries, businesses, or schools are given a totally different range of communicative energy than that extended to family members. The most energy, of course, is either given or withheld from our immediate family members. As small children, we learn initially to give most of our emotional communication to our parents and our siblings. The experiences we record as we interrelate with each member of the family are stored and referenced subconsciously, so that later in life we may experience a familiar feeling that is associated with mothering, or sibling rivalry, or paternal discipline, and we unconsciously project these old channels onto that person with whom we are now relating.

As we grow older and the ego becomes more combative and discriminating, we often expend a great deal of energy withholding communication from our close family members as we attempt to separate from them, thinking erroneously that we will have more energy for ourselves and be stronger if we are not attached. This is truly the case between teenagers and parents, where the pattern of communication becomes one of resistance; the parent is insisting or pressing against the teenager, who feels that the self cannot be expressed while there is still an emotional tie to the parents. The young person has long since become focused on the peer group and resists the parents' attempts at communication.

There is often a similar pattern with sisters and brothers, whereby, initially, a lot of attention was shared by each child. As they grow and attempt to define their own worlds and their own power within the family, they begin to take up an unconscious attitude that says, "Since I need the attention, I will give no attention to my sibling."

Early on, children learn from their parents an expediency in relationship, a capacity to categorize those who are important, those who must receive energy from us, those we can ignore, those who are not as powerful as we, those from whom we need something or want something, and those whom we should avoid. These feelings are the seeds of relationships of limitation that we enact in later life. Though we are supposedly partners in life, emotionally we are still entrapped in the search to be fulfilled by others. We weigh and measure what is ours and what we must relinquish in order to get what we want, while expending as little energy as possible.

We learn to perceive appropriate energy exchanges, not intellectually or mentally, but through the magnificent communication capacities of our auric fields and our psychic intuitive faculties. This conscious perception is truly the great inheritance of our species. We have not five senses, not six, but more than seventy senses that can help us recognize each other on very profound levels. If a parent is cueing a child that a person is of value and is important, the communication is picked up by the subtle perceptions of these invisible senses. The nuances of approval, of love, of closeness, are actually sensory perceptions that the child learns, even before birth!

CHANNEL CATEGORIES

Categories of relationship contain almost infinite variations of the main channels such as brother, buddy, lover, father, mother, teacher, friend, advocate, enemy. There are also the senses of energy flow between people in relationship, such as less than, more than, owed to, received from. Through experiencing these boxes, we have compiled thousands of sensory cues that allow us to categorize communication and respond with the quality of energy that relates to each—a buddy relationship as opposed to a lover relationship, for example.

If I were to say to you, "Close your eyes and feel the presence of a buddy kind of energy. You and I are buddies. We support each other. Let yourself sense our trusting, playful buddy energy," you would be able to feel exactly what that energy is. Yet if I asked you to describe it, your descriptive phrases might not convey the real meaning, because the words *warmness* or *trust*, when applied to specific relationships such as buddy trust or lover trust, might have totally different nuances.

How would you describe the sense of trust? If you were describing it in a linear, mental way, it would be just one flat reference point. As soon as it is attached to another person, it takes on entirely new sensations. Trust of a lover, a child, a colleague: each has a different emotional scenario; yet there is a special energy that you can discern that says, "This is the buddy vibration." If you were an actor in a play, and you were to enact a role in which you were someone's buddy, you would be able to do it clearly and easily so that the audience could experience it as exactly that buddy ray of energy.

Not only would you be using all your psychic, intuitive cues, but your body would be expressing itself in a particular way of comforting with no pretense. When a potential lover comes into your presence, however, you would be on alert immediately and the body would begin to make gestures that perhaps conform to a recognizable universal pattern of expression that conveys a sexual awareness. For example, you might smile a certain way or use your eyes to gesture, to communicate the openness of your body on the sexual level. Sexual nuance is one of the easiest channels to recognize because it is so integral to the body.

When a parent is present in front of you, the body's gestures, communication, and expressions would be totally different. Next time you are with your parents, observe how your body expresses your subconscious feelings about who you are in the relationship. How do you hold your head? Do you hold on to your body or cross your arms and legs? These gestures show timidity and self-protection. Do you often stand with your legs apart, hands on hips, or behind the head? These are poses of will and superiority.

Each channel brings forth a different kind of tension that comes from the body, depending on the quality and intensity of the relationship. Becoming aware of these channels of relations and of how you learn to use them is one of the most fascinating aspects of communication. All these channels of communication that describe your relationship with any particular being can become conscious choices, and you can alter or correct a channel to reflect what you really want to experience. Ultimately you will learn to integrate the channels so that your relationships become truly holographic; the lover, the teacher, the friend, can be used in concert to amplify a relationship, as all enhance the experience of merging with another person.

FACILITATOR/CLIENT CHANNELS

When you first meet a person, you encounter the challenge of discerning the right channel of communication. A sense of comfort sets in as soon as you have established a sense of order. In the Western world, the totem-pole structure is common in most social and interpersonal relationships. This is characterized by a vertical line of dominance in which someone is classified as above or below you and then related to in terms of those fixed positions of relationship. It is amazing to discover that, on the level of the soul, you can relate without structural guidelines. By becoming aware of how fluent you actually are in this language of relation categorization, you can use or dissolve it to increase the potential of your relationships and the clarity of your communication with anyone.

At the Light Institute, a great deal of the facilitator training is related to the art of invisibility, whereby the facilitator must learn how to bring about a level of communication with the client that does not fall into any of these stereotyped categories. The facilitator does not choose to be the great, wise teacher or the loving mother, or the buddy-friend, or the formal professional, or the parent with the child. None of these categories will give the optimum result when working on profound spiritual levels. Communication between the facilitator and the client becomes a communication of the heart—not the emotional, sympathetic heart, but the all-knowing, all-loving heart of the Higher Self that is expressed by the facilitator incorporating a level of invisibility that does not invite projection on the part of the client but, rather, fosters the meeting between the client and the Higher Self. The facilitator is merely the instrument of the Higher Self to guide the client into scenarios and awakenings that speed enlightenment.

At the Light Institute, we learn how to scan the channels in the same way that a person might scan the radio channels to pick up exactly the right program or the right energy that someone wishes to attune or listen to. In the same way, when we are communicating with someone, we can use our understanding of these different points of reference to help each other become comfortable and familiar. We all recognize that vibration of openness we call "friend," and perhaps there are times when someone reaches out to us on the partnership channel, asking for a lover, and we may answer back from the channel of friend.

When we are clear about our intention or our choice, we can communicate very clearly to anyone around us exactly what those intentions or choices are. One of the areas in which many people support dishonesty within themselves is in not acknowledging responsibility for these subtle messages that are sent out through our auric field. By our tone of voice and body posture, we cue others to our feelings about them in a way that is so much safer for us than actually speaking aloud those intentions or feelings (which we might not want to acknowledge) This causes a great deal of confusion and clutters the channels of relationship between ourselves and others.

FEMININE AND MASCULINE CHANNELS

There are feminine channels and masculine channels of relationships that are easily identifiable because of the obvious style of each. A feminine channel may be soft and passive, supportive and submissive, or, conversely, manipulative and cajoling; a masculine channel may be more direct, controlling, authoritarian, externalized, and content- or goal-oriented. You learn to pick these channels in accordance with the style of communication that expresses your identity as male or female. Your Emotional Body carries all of what you have learned as a child about being safe in order to survive, and it will freeze you within one or the other dominant channel instead of merging the two. Often people continue to support these separate channels of communication simply because those are the repertoires that the Emotional Body remembers and therefore likes to reexperience.

The feminine and masculine energies are not just random energies inherited from parents or picked up on the great psychic network to which you attune socially and culturally; they are recorded, living essence energies coming from the magnificent repertory of your soul. Your soul actually does know what it is like to be a male or a female, and it remembers what experiences it has had expressing and growing through each of those two channels. In your many incarnations, you have been both male and female, and the residues of those bodies and experiences are present within each cell, which has inherited experiential history.

At the Light Institute, the Inner Male and the Inner Female energetics are acknowledged as complete encapsulations of experiences that the soul has had in either male or female body. Because of the lessons and imprints of those experiences that are still resonating within you, your present reality is very much influenced by them. Once you come into contact with the memories of the Inner Male and the Inner Female, they become a powerful channel reconnecting you with the masculine and feminine, yin/yang essence energies, which are beyond the history of embodied experience in terms of content but, rather, describe and activate those energies in their pure universal form.

The masculine and feminine channels have different functional applications. For example, you may use the feminine channel to access a creative endeavor or explore a relationship. If, however, you are hoping someone will accept an idea you have, you are much more likely to be commanding or to speak in a formal, masculine voice in order to bluff a sense of dominance that might bring the other person into agreement with you. This you might do not out of a sense of commonality as much as out of the intent to engender fear so that you can gain the upper hand. These habits of persuasion through control are the bases of the negative patterns of communication between whole nations on this planet; if they are dissolved on the personal level, they will be altered on the global level as well.

A powerful exercise in awareness is to contemplate each interchange you have had and observe which channel you were using. Very quickly you will begin to perceive your own personal male/female balance. How you use each will give you a profound look into your Emotional Body's view of who you are.

CROSS CHANNELS

Not only do you develop certain habitual channels, but you pick and choose from your own personal repertoire, to become the male with one person, the female with another, the child or the teacher, as it suits your purposes. These can be excellent skills if you are aware of them, but very often your purpose, from the Emotional Body's perspective, is simply to be safe or to survive. The Emotional Body therefore often misuses these skills by pretending roles rather than speaking from the channel of the heart. Until the Emotional Body is clear, it experiences great difficulty in embracing the "honest" heart.

It is fascinating to observe ourselves actually using these different energies in order to communicate. Often, when we are trying to understand why we have difficulties in certain relationships, if we look at our communications in those relationships we can see that the interference is coming from the different roles being played. There is a cross-channeling effect in which we misalign our frequencies with others, resulting in surprising interplays between us. For example, a man may tend to project onto his wife and treat her as if she were his mother, relating to her from his little-boy channel. Women often set up this kind of relationship with their lovers because it allows them a measure

of safety or control. A woman might use her little-girl channel
to respond to her husband as if he were her father in order to
continue to feel protected and to elicit nurturing feelings from
him.

These crossover channels become even more complicated
when our inner personalities start relating to each other. For
example, if you are a man, the masculine channel is the obvious
one for you to use. However, when relating to a woman, you
may be communicating with her inner male energy. Thus, it is
actually the two men who are struggling with each other, whereas
the physical female and the physical male really love each other!
So often people say, "We fight all the time, but we do care."

I call this subconscious polarity energy (which corresponds
with the four main channels) the *Inner Male, Inner Female,
Inner Parents,* and *Inner Child.* When we appear to be one thing
yet emotionally play out the attributes of another, we are engaging
in levels of projection that defy communication. The friction that
results can be that of any combination—between the parent and
child roles, or the male energy residing in the woman competing
with the male energy residing in the man, or the female energy
in the man bouncing off the female energy in the woman!

One of the major problems in relationships comes from a
sense of competition rather than cooperation. We do this in order
to get our way or to influence the other. Who is actually fighting?
It could be the two males: the Inner Male of the female chal-
lenging the man, competing for dominance. It could be the Inner
Female of one attempting to control the other female. It could
be the two Inner Children who are vying to have their needs
met, each demanding that the other relinquish its demands in
order to take care of the needs of the other one.

It is common in many families to have one child who plays
the parent or the peacekeeper, the one who negotiates for peace
within the family. If a child has learned that the safe position in
the family is to carry out the role of the parent, that will become
the overriding repertoire of his personality, so that when the
person becomes an adult, he will continually play out that role

with everyone he meets. This may be appropriate with some people. With others it may cause discomfort and imbalance in the relationship because the channel in which he is most comfortable simply may not match another's channels of communication. Instead of welcoming the strength his partner is projecting in an attempt to make him feel safe, the other person may feel that he is being treated like a child. In this case the peacekeeper may be using these techniques to control rather than to communicate.

For example, a woman who has been taught to play the mother may find difficulties in attracting a male who is strong enough to be her partner. She may go through a series of relationships with men who are seeking mothers and for whom she continually must take responsibility. Ultimately she comes to feel resentment that there is no man willing to give her that adult kind of relationship, never being aware that she is not attracting those kinds of men because the channel she is using is only attracting males who need to be mothered!

Sometimes as individuals grow, they move into roles that are helpful to their own balance but are not compatible with their partners. A woman might begin to explore the masculine energy while her husband begins to long for the safety of childhood. The male in her may become impatient with the child. These are the relationships at cross-purposes that are so common. If the man is given the opportunity to hear his Inner Child, he may again be ready to express his love as a man or a father. By contacting the Inner Child, he can revisit the pure energy that is in communion with the soul and so remember the power of the child, rather than the third-dimensional need to be parented.

Someone who wants to play the protective father, or who was forced or taught to do so as a child, may have developed a self-image that corresponds only with that one channel of communication. Eventually he will feel sucked dry from having everyone turn to him to answer all needs and solve all problems. He needs to experience that he can become the receiver and thus find peace by being given help and love.

As we become whole in our Emotional Body and expand our awareness to use more channels of communication, our relationships will go through powerful changes. When women are able to enjoy the powerful aspects of feminine psyche, the intuition, the nurturing, the capacity to be a companion, they begin to enjoy each other's company rather than competing.

The cosmic giggle comes into play when two women compete for a man by engaging the yang or masculine aspects of themselves to outmaneuver each other. Eventually they must recognize cosmic truth and realize that relationships cannot be won. Instead they come to us through our choice to experience them. We choose love or the lack of it by our emotional and karmic inclinations; the relationship is not the quest, but only the backdrop for the lesson of the soul. Competition for love is an old, outdated thought form that gives us motivation for new lessons. All too often the man for whom two women compete is really only an incidental aspect of a battle in which the "other woman" is the principal to whom one is relating! Now is the opportunity for women to use the Inner Male in more rewarding and creative ways.

The same is true, of course, for men together. Men tragically limit the depth of their relationships with one another because they feel that they must uphold their habit of competition to continually ascertain manhood, dominance, and the facade of independence. They pretend this to each other only, as women know very well how easily men become dependent.

When a man is able to express his feminine qualities, his psychic, intuitive qualities, to another man, there is a potential for a much deeper and rewarding relationship. Can you imagine what will happen to the world when men actually turn their attention away from their external focus and communicate from their nurturing, creative, feminine levels? The desire to find this kind of intimacy is one of the factors in the rise of homosexuality—a need to rebalance the overt male with the inner expression of the female. Men are beginning to turn that energy back to themselves. They suffer because of the socially imposed alicnation from their Emotional Body. The superficial levels of communication left open to them, which only allow discussion of their exterior presentation in the world, cause them great stress. The pressure-cooker effect of withholding true feelings is taking its toll on men around the world.

When a man no longer needs to uphold a constrictive stereotype of who he is or what he will receive from anyone outside him, he can let go of the limitations that impede his growth and his fulfillment. When men are willing to share with each other on a soul level, there will no longer be war on this planet. As these yang energies are tempered by an upsurge in creative expression, we will be able to smooth out destructive energies by retuning the channel of our communication to one that has less static, that can be received clearly by the other.

It is up to mothers and female partners to relieve this imbalance by helping men expand their channels of communication to include their inner emotional and spiritual worlds. The only danger with this comes from the female who has shut off her own Inner Female and become cynical of energy expression because she has been taught that emotional expression denotes weakness. Therefore, she is afraid of her own emotions and will become anxious if she views this trait in a male partner. Such a relationship will be doomed to dryness and will probably fail. She must discover the connection between inner feelings and divine essence.

In fact, women hunger for a man who will share his tender side, his feminine self. Most women find this self-disclosure very exciting and appealing. Such emotions lead to a deeper commonality of spirit. This is a higher octave of the woman-to-woman channel; it is the divine/feminine channel merging with itself.

If you are in a man's body and are not allowing that Inner Female to be seen, you are cut off from an energy that is a predominant aspect of your own hidden self. By seeking out the Inner Female through the channels of perception rather than through the mind, you can learn to access these energies and wield them in a way that enriches the choices you have for relationship as well as the expression of your Divine Self. The Inner Male or the Inner Female seeks expression and covertly influences your communication with the outside world. The more unconscious you are of these energies, the more confusion you may experience emotionally in your life.

A woman who is carrying memories of the Inner Female in which there was, perhaps, a fear in birthing or a negative experience in expressing her feminine energy, may unconsciously deny that feminine energy within so that she compensates by expressing herself within the masculine format as aggressive, mental, or argumentative. Her subconscious memory of the feminine power may include an experience in which expressing it caused her death. Her emotional and physical bodies will both have recordings of this, and without knowing why, she will resist coming into contact with that energy so that she can avoid reexperiencing the negative memories that have become conclusions on the part of her subconscious. Until she has a way of revisiting the experiences of the Emotional Body, she cannot change her unconscious feelings. They will simply override any tendencies she might have toward those feminine knowings, those feminine energies.

It is clear that different individuals have specific personalized hormonal systems and that often many of the difficulties we have within our urinary-genital or reproductive tracts seem to relate to subtle hormonal imbalances. Science has no way of observing what is influencing the endocrine system to release those hormones that affect our personalities and our emotions, as well as our physical bodies. Yet here is one of those truths—if the yin energy is allowed, then the body, too, will follow suit and secrete the hormones that are related to feminine expression. But if there is fear or denial of that feminine energy, the body will withhold biochemical influences that would enhance the expression of an energy that is viewed by the unconscious as dangerous.

This is why it is so important to use consciousness to influence how your body will receive any medication you take, such as any hormonal support that changes the emotional balance on spiritual, physiological, or even mental levels. It is crucial that the body receives a message allowing it to feel that the secretion of hormones that alter the male/female balances is within the safekeeping of its own guidelines.

You have your own personal mix of masculine/feminine energies that are expressed physically, emotionally, and spiritually. These are not thrust upon you but are designed by your own soul to aid you in your journey to universal consciousness. If you begin to watch the channels of relation you select for different people in your life, you will come to know these energies intimately and be able to discard the habits of mismatching. By simply changing the channel in relationships of discord, you can experience knowing, and you will be able to communicate with them as if they were totally new people in your life!

5

THE ONES WITHIN

All your unconscious memories of other lifetimes and the associations you have to different bodies are rich resource material for the expression of who you are right now. For example, you have always identified yourself in terms of your place in a family: mother, father, child, male, or female. These are not just roles, but actual energetics that shape your behavior and expression. I call them *Inner Entities* because they are like real people or aspects living within your body. You can come to know them intimately by exploring your many incarnations.

If you contemplate the meaning of these multi-incarnational memories, you must begin to see that your current primary relationships can also be used as an opportunity to discover the memories and imprints of your soul's journey. For example, as you become aware of the dilemmas of being a parent, you begin to view your own parents with compassion. You may have felt separate from your parents, but if you explore your own repertoire of parenting, you will be able to comprehend and rebalance the essence energies acted out through these various roles, from within. These Inner Entities lead to myriad expressive choices that include the Inner Father, the Inner Mother, the Inner Male, and the Inner Female.

All of these singular energies can be plucked from the fabric of your consciousness and be reintegrated in vital ways that change your reality. Becoming aware that there is a living polarity body (or energetic opposite gender) within each of us was the most transformative awakening that I have experienced. It has an immediate effect on personality structure, behavior, and habits, as well as the deep spiritual recognition of the true self. It is such a relief to give yourself permission to express the feelings you held inside while others were free to enact your own longings.

Using this multi-incarnational format for recognizing these energies creates a profound transformational opportunity because you can expand your consciousness through an actual experience. This is great fun! Just as when you were a child and tried on all the costumes you could, trying on lifetimes gives you the same power to discard or choose feelings, talents, and character traits that truly suit you while consciously discarding those that don't. You can use all your senses to feel and acknowledge energies that are otherwise projected outside yourself onto others. A fantastic integration of subconscious feelings and thought forms takes place through unlimited arcs of association that come together synchronistically and synergistically when you stretch your sense of yourself outside the confines of just one lifetime view. You can access the experiences of being mother, father, male, and female to more deeply absorb the dynamics of self-expression. Thus, if you are in a female body, there is a male and a father within you as well. When you ask the Inner Male or the Inner Female to take form and allow yourself to be shown and participate in the experiences you have collected in each of those lifetimes, you feel the tingle of life that helps you know who you truly are!

Exploring your Inner Entities will open you to the hidden dynamics of emotional projection. You can have an intimate look into the realities of each body instead of just the projection you have created by witnessing them from outside. It is fascinating to see how you relate to the experiences in lifetimes with the same gender of body you have now, as opposed to lifetimes in which you had the opposite gender body with all its specific themes. You will feel very different about the opposite sex when you have lived in that body.

A major theme for women, for example, is abandonment. When they see this scenario from the experience of the male, they begin to understand how women actually push men into abandoning them. They rarely look deep enough to acknowledge that they subconsciously wanted to be alone or needed the opportunity to evolve their own yang force. Without the balancing of masculine experience, the female will tend to imprint helplessness and depression as she retreats into the formless aspects of feminine energy. When she is reliving all her female experiences, she has a tendency to become enmeshed in a one-sided reality that recapitulates all the struggles and female points of view. As these are brought to consciousness, however, they can be released so that true feminine power and grace begin to surface and influence her experiences now.

The same is true for the man flushing out the imprints of his male bodies. Without the balancing of the female perspective, he will extend the yang energy to that of the ultimate killer or feel it fall in upon itself with the despair of impotence. Impotence occurs because there is no inner structure (feminine energy) to support the outer thrust. If there is no inner energy of the opposite sex, the external representation is empty. In Chinese medicine we call it *empty chi.* It means that the external representation has no life force of its own. It is like the paper tiger pretending something that it is not.

When the woman accesses the Inner Male, she begins to shine and exude confidence because she is able to bring forth those deep secrets she didn't know she had inside and give them full expression. The man embracing his Inner Female touches something every human being longs for: the intuitive knowings that allow us to give from the heart and surrender our defenses enough to truly receive love.

This seems to be the divine whispering of our species—that male and female must come together, fuse, and re-form in endless

THE ONES WITHIN • 65

variations and potentials of expression. It is a new concept that our merging could be one of creativity rather than mere dependence.

When your Emotional Body is no longer dependent on someone outside you, your recognition of who they are alters completely. For the first time, you are able to see them as a flawless whole being, rather than as the extension of something you cannot reach inside yourself and therefore need to criticize or seduce. The self-sufficient person, the whole person, has the abundance to love and is free from the buying and selling so characteristic of relationship. Through discovery of these gender experiences, many of the judgments and fears about the opposite sex are dissolved.

Let us participate in the exercise of looking at our Inner Female so that we can allow this energy full range as it modifies, enhances, and enriches the expression of the masculine.

The first time you do this exercise, it is appropriate to be alone and to have a little time to go into an in-depth exploration, to allow the subconscious imprints to rise to the surface. Once you have made contact with the Inner Female, she becomes a living essence, a living part of you, and you can call forth her energy to help you at any time.

EXERCISE FOR COMMUNION WITH THE INNER FEMALE

Close your eyes. Take a deep breath, breathing in the light, and as you exhale, feel that you are exhaling all the thoughts that have filled your head, that have taken up your awareness, so that each time you take a deep breath, you feel more and more empty of thoughts and feelings. The more empty you become, the more expanded you are. Become aware that you are filling the entire space of the room, and when you can experience that sense of expansion, simply ask

your Inner Female, the female within, to take form. Accept
the first form that you sense or see or hear.

She may appear initially in symbolic form, such as a
flower or a waterfall. She may be some kind of woman or
mystical being. Accept the form as an expression of feminine
energy as she is living within you now.

Once you perceive your Inner Female, feel the quality
of her energy. Is she masterful or frightened? Just feel the
kind of energy that is coming from her and surrounding
you. Breathe that energy in so that it pervades your every
cell.

Ask the Inner Female to touch your body. See where she
touches you. And at that point of contact, allow all your
senses to come to focus, to come to rest, so that you feel the
quality of the touch, the temperature, the pressure, what
happens in your body when you are touched by her.

When she has made contact with you through her touch,
ask her what gift she needs from you to be balanced in your
life now. You will get a telepathic answer or even see a symbol
or an object or color that she is asking for. Draw that gift into
the top of your head as if it is coming from the universe and
extend it out to her from your stomach or solar plexus area.
Notice where she takes it into her body and observe how it
changes her.

Now, ask her to give you a gift represented by a symbol,
an object, or a color that will integrate her into your conscious
life. It might be a smell. It might be a sound, a color, or
some object that has profound meaning in your psyche. You
may not understand the meaning of the gifts at all. It does
not matter if your linear mind understands. Simply ask for
the gift that will create the integration of her into your life.
The moment you sense that gift, draw it into your body and
notice exactly where it comes in.

When it comes into your body, feel it there in that part,
and then, as if you could make a replica, a picture of it in
every one of the trillions of cells in your body, record that

gift in every cell of the body. When you feel that gift inside you, notice the shifting of energy within you, any feelings or sensations that you may have.

Now, draw the Inner Female into your body and simply feel your body opening and bringing her into you. Pay attention to where and how she enters your body.

Notice how you feel more alive when you experience the Inner Female, consciously, as a part of you!

Sometimes people have had negative experiences in female form, and the Inner Female may reflect the imprinting of those experiences by appearing in a disturbing way, such as an old hag, witch, or threatening animal. Don't worry about this; just give her a gift and watch her transmute her negative form. It is, however, wonderful to explore those negative experiences and imprints by doing multi-incarnational work that will dissolve all the residues. Each time you work with your Inner Female, the energy in your body will become stronger and clearer and you will discover how many more choices of expression you have in your body and your life than you had previously realized.

A WOMAN AND HER INNER MALE

A woman's most deeply held impressions of men come from the patterning she learns as a small girl from her mother. If the mother demurs, manipulates, despises, or undercuts her husband, the little girl will grow to do the same. If her mother teaches her that women are limited in scope, she may try to emulate men from her earliest childhood so as to find a way to express her need for power.

Often, the masculine pretends itself through the force of anger, passive aggressiveness, or overt thrust. As it comes forward in the female, she may use it only to strike out or to angrily spew her energy. Having always hidden her true self, she may be overly forceful when clearing her yang force. This soon passes if she can direct this energy into something where it can burn in a focused way, such as physical or creative activity.

The female separated from the male in herself may also experience all the fear of abandonment and helplessness because she does not recognize that she can protect or accomplish on her own. This is a kind of yin impotence that creates depression and inertia. Interestingly, the powerful instinctual protectiveness of mothering will often distract her from these feelings as her attention is diverted to her young. This is especially the case after divorce when she may feel abandoned but is forced to take on the masculine role for her family.

A most amazing transformation takes place in a woman who has experienced her Inner Male—all the attributes and qualities she hungers for in the male outside her can be addressed from within her. The actual experience of having the strength or the capacity to protect, or to manifest abundance or be the initiator of action or the source of teaching, or to have any of the multitudinous attributes she seeks in her male partner and finds, suddenly, within her own self, frees her from her dependence patterns with the males in her life.

Many women are afraid of men. Experiencing themselves in a male body helps them lose their fear of being overwhelmed by physical size or by some lurking sexual potential. Accessing their Inner Male quite naturally teaches them how to "reach" men on levels that count. For example, a woman who is fearful of male dominance may discover that she, herself, wearing the body of a male in some other lifetime, has dominated or destroyed females, and that residue is the source of her mistrust of the males in her life now. She cannot trust the Inner Male with whom she has intimate, if subconscious, awareness of destructive potential.

When she releases those experiences of the Inner Male literally by washing them from the cells of her body, she is free to interact with the males in her life without any hidden agendas relating to survival or control. As she learns to love and use her

Inner Male, she greatly amplifies her capacity to love all other males. She will begin to select masculine energies and personalities around her that reflect the highest qualities of yang energy. By clearing away her negative experiences in male body, she will ultimately come to lifetimes in which she has exquisitely used the power of the yang force for the good. By so remembering those powerful, positive qualities, she becomes a healing catalyst of morphic resonance and psychic communication that facilitates all the males on this planet to resonate to a higher understanding of the masculine force.

A WOMAN AND HER INNER FEMALE

It is fascinating for a woman to experience the Inner Female. Many of the attributes of her female energy are occulted or locked within the subconscious in order to protect her from herself. Perhaps she holds some fearful memory of the result of expressing that Inner Female. The last two-thousand-year cycle has not been easy for women. From birthing to growing and serving, to surviving the hostilities of body and spirit, the female has had to develop some fairly subversive tactics for existing in a world uncaring or unaware of her special needs. As she explores her entire repertoire of feminine experience, these themes begin to translate themselves into subconscious material that is a part of her present makeup, applicable to her present experience. Buried in the "past" lies the source of the adaptive techniques that must be cleared in order for her to live now with honesty and power.

Many nuances of the physical body are expressed through these multi-incarnational experiences, so that the female is able to see directly the correlation between how she feels about her body now and the residues she is carrying from so many feminine lifetimes. She can re-create or restructure herself by shifting these energies and releasing those that are slowing her growth. By clearing away the negative experiences of abuse, neglect, pain, and death she has had in other female lifetimes, she strengthens her body, which is thus renewed and available for the imprints of prestige and dignity. Because she discovers that the feminine energy is profoundly connected to the creative source so needed in today's world, her sense of security and delight in being in feminine body is greatly enhanced.

As her feminine repertoire expands, she becomes powerful in her expression of the female because she is, after all, backed by so many lifetimes; it is as if she had been handed the collective experience of all women, simply through her own multi-incarnational history. She becomes the true expert, magician, and alchemist of these feminine energies, which then can so easily mingle and resonate with the energies she is carrying now.

One of the major themes that women must deal with relates to the illusion that they would have been more abundant, more powerful, more free, had they been born in the body of a male. But when a woman is able to comb through an infinite variety of expression of feminine power and knowing, she begins to understand from the depth of her being what it means to be female. Inevitably, she finds lifetimes in which she has been powerful or free as a female. These resources, which were given to her by virtue of her innate feminine orientation, become available to increase the magnitude of her expression.

Acceptance and surrender are two powerful allies of creative expression. When you commit yourself to using the body that you have, that body begins to perform in magical ways, and your experience of your own potential is maximized.

A MAN AND HIS INNER MALE

When a man experiences his Inner Male, he is able to call forth a tremendous wealth of energy for manifestation or "doing." He begins to express all the themes that have to do with visibility, structure, wisdom, or form. Over the centuries, the expression of masculine energy has modified itself from that of brute strength (which was once acceptable or even necessary) to a much more subtle expression of dominance. Body memories of rougher days may influence behavior and bring embarrassment to the man who has trouble suppressing the old residues. For example, a man who wrestles with his temper may find other lifetimes in which his power to survive was dependent on his capacity to overwhelm or direct. Those attributes may have aided his success as well as that of others and thus be inextricably mixed with his subconscious yet self-righteous sense of himself. To be the leader meant to command, direct, or possibly even to force. Those techniques and attitudes may not meet with the same success or acceptance from those in present-day society who require him to become more mental or more subtle and less forceful in his expression. However, by revisiting his success, whether on a physical or some other level, he will be able to use that powerful energy now, without the old style of force. The quality of leadership can become his natural gift.

A MAN AND HIS INNER FEMALE

A common fear as well as an actual experience of men today is impotence—impotence on sexual, emotional, and other levels. Often this comes because the yang, masculine energy is only part of an external expression that does not carry with it an inner sense that the man is as powerful as he pretends. He may secretly believe that he has no real core within him that can sustain the thrust of his pretensions.

The female energy heals the spirit of pretense with its gentle ability to focus on the other person and experience what he or she is experiencing. The moment the man lets go of his mental fears and begins to feel the energetics of the bodies with his sensual feminine essence, the natural functions of the body take over. It is ironic that the feminine qualities of perception are the antidote for failure to perform on masculine levels, when it was the fear of not being manly enough that so influenced the malfunction in the first place!

The most immediately evident transformation comes after sessions in which men experience the feminine energy within them. It is an energy that they have had stripped away because of cultural descriptions of what is male and what is female. Having had all the recesses of feminine expression either filtered out or actively removed from them by the time they reach adulthood, men have a most profound spiritual and emotional experience when they rediscover a reservoir of that feminine energy still intact, deeply within.

When a man has restricted himself to the yang expression, never showing his tenderness or emotions, never accessing the yin energy within him, he will return to the child within when reintroduced to his deeper feelings, because that is the reference point of his gentleness. If he has been isolated into the yang energy, he will have a strong need to experience the Inner Female through which he can rebalance his give-and-take with the world. Sometimes the Inner Female is imprinted in such a damaged, vulnerable, or frail way that he feels desperate not to return to her energy. The thought form may have been, "If I express my yin, I will not survive." As the yin energies flood into his consciousness, the capacity to select memories that can open these currents of feeling may rearrange even the personality itself. He finds that he may now express tenderness in relationships because he can replace those fearful memories with ones that have brought him great fulfillment. But he must learn to express the yin energy not only from the position of the adult, but also from the strength of the spiritual. He can open the floodgates of this powerful essence energy through meditation, the Higher Self, and directly through the Inner Female.

THE INNER PARENT

At the Light Institute, the second series of sessions we do with clients is devoted to the clearing of the parents. We explore the lifetimes you have had with them so that you understand exactly why you chose parents who would contribute to your physical form as well as to your emotional, spiritual, and mental makeup by passing on those qualities that would provide that certain arena of growth. Following the clearing of the external people in your life upon whom you project, such as your parents, you have a perfect opportunity to work on the Inner Parent, the parent within.

When you experience mothering or fathering energy as something outside yourself, you are projecting and seeing yourself in the mirror of your parents. This is the self of the personality, the ego—the self that is surviving, weighing, measuring, evaluating, and judging itself through its relationship to or reflection from the parents.

When you begin to explore your Inner Father and Inner Mother, you are setting the stage for divine energy to take up residence in your body so that all the characteristics and realities of the parent can be experienced from inside yourself. You must relinquish the addiction to the "damaged child" syndrome, whereby you judge your potential on the restrictions and hardships placed upon you by your parents. The spiritual acknowledgment of having chosen your parents frees you from this emotional entrapment and moves you on to the power and wisdom of your choice on the level of soul. Direct, multi-incarnational contact with your parents leads to compassion and recognition of spiritual realities, rather than emotional projections.

By viewing your own inner experiences of the parent, you establish a relationship with the unmanifest that creates the space for expansion, completely transforming the way your body, your personality, and even your soul are able to move in relationship to the outside world. You are redesigning your place in the world because you have so extended your experience, your frame of reference that could communicate with the world. This work creates a point of clarity, a centering, which is immovable because it is not created out of the need to mirror or the suffering of polarity in reaction to the outside world. It is literally the still point through which the soul builds a center within your physical self that nourishes and supports the purpose of life and, therefore, the progression of your soul.

Exploration of the Inner Parent is an electrifying awakening to the knowledge of the bondage of culture. It leads you from the constriction of cultural attitudes back to the pure essences of parenting that contribute to the success of our species. As you begin to see the experiences and thought forms by which you identify the energy of your Inner Parents, you can strip away the collective as well as the individual imprints that have been laid down within the genetic codes, that have to do with survival, success, or permission. The manner in which these innermost essence energies are expressed becomes clarified and purified.

For example, a person may have imprints having to do with the qualifications for being a good father. As we explore the different cultures in which the person has experienced being a father, we are able to clear away those imprints, which are simply the thought forms of particular cultures and may, in fact, be contradictory to each other or inappropriate precepts to meet the future. In one culture a father may be held separate from his children or may never express his love for them verbally, but only through complicated rituals or life-style patterns that express his caring for his family. It may be that his extended family is as important as the individual family. In another culture, the father may be the one who nurtures the child.

In some cultures, as the woman labors, the father physically experiences the labor pains for the mother. In El Salvador, which was a one-crop country at the time I lived there, the men stayed home and took care of the children when it was not coffee-picking time, while the women traveled far and wide, occupying themselves in a variety of different kinds of trading activities to support the family.

As people experience several different cultural and even racial perspectives of parenting, they come more deeply into the essence energy that has to do with the quality of parental love. The way love is expressed becomes much less important as they are able to see that, no matter the outside ritual or behavior patterns, the deeper essence parenting energy is what is important to the soul. The more widely they have experienced parenting, the more successful they are as parents and as human beings no matter what cultural behaviors are used. Thus the Brazilian, the Russian, and the African dissolve into an energetic matrix that allows a broader spectrum of the parenting experience and the expression of love between souls.

When you are experiencing the Inner Parent, you are looking for these kinds of threads or essence materials. You discover how it was for you in all your incarnations to be the parent—the mother, the father. How did you pass down to your offspring those imprints that taught them to parent? Which of those imprints limit you and your children in terms of experiencing parenting energy now?

By releasing and even remixing them, you are helping the entire genetic pool of this planet to dissolve the complexities that create confusion and separation. By so doing, you are strengthening the access to the spiritual source that belongs to us all and bringing it into conscious proximity so that future parenting will be experienced as an expression of the divine.

When you touch these energies of pure love, of the capacity to nurture and teach, to embrace all the other elements of parenting, you begin to experience radiance and unconditional love rather than reactive, limited responses or learned behavior patterns that limit the soul's expression.

BIRTHING FOR THE MAN

Working with the opposite or polarity body is very rewarding because of the way it creates holographic or interconnected reference points as to who you are and how you express and communicate to your children. One of the most profound experiences available to men is to feel themselves giving birth. Throughout the ages there has been so much mystery and ritual surrounding birth that it has played a central role in the separation and hostility between males and females. The masculine force, being unable to participate in birth, has used its aggressive, dominating energy to pretend that birth is not something as mysterious and special as it actually is. In today's world men have overlaid this mystery with the instruments of technology to ensure their place at birth, literally contorting it rather than surrendering to the mystery of spirit, the mystery of the soul's choice to be born. Birthing is an experience that women must reclaim and then learn to share with men so they can experience it, not from the imbalance of control, but from the feminine principle of inclusion that can participate in the mystery of birth.

When men experience the Inner Mother session at the Light Institute, the facilitator elongates or puts into slow motion the birthing process so that they can become familiar with it on a physical level as well as on emotional and spiritual levels. This is tremendously helpful for men who are going to become birthing partners to their wives, because when they have a frame of reference for the experience, they are so much more eager to help their partner.

I feel the experience of awakening the cells' birthing memories is one of the most emotional and rewarding for men. It is one that often causes them truly to let go in their emotional and physical bodies; to cry and to become ecstatic, to feel that they are somehow rejoined with their spiritual source. It is the feminine aspect of the divine, from which they have been so cut off that often they have not been able to feel their spiritual energy. There is something so godly and sacred in giving birth and being the vehicle of new and perfect life, nurturing that perfect life. Men never forget it!

It is especially wonderful for a man who was somehow disconnected from the love of his mother, perhaps in a technological world where he was not nursed or held or bonded to his mother. The experience as he lies upon the table, as he describes himself suckling a baby, and the feelings in the body that are available to him actually heal that longing that he cannot seem to heal in any other way. These feelings of not being loved or welcomed or nurtured dissolve as he becomes the nurturer, the one who welcomes the new being. This is, in fact, a sound cosmic principle of energy: We heal ourselves by healing others. We receive by giving. Within the heart of every human is a profound desire to give, to contribute, to be needed. This experience of being the mother reunites males with the sacred mystery of life and inevitably reconnects with them their own spirituality in a way previously unachievable, because for so many, spirituality is couched in the confines of religions, in the mental body of dogma, rather than in the pure energy that we are all hungry for on the cellular level.

So many men stifle a competitive urge or a hopeless sense of separation and unworthiness at the birth of their own children when the mother and the baby bond into a new "couple" as a result of nursing. When a man has experienced himself in that role, he is able to join in the joy at the birth of his child, rather than experiencing any negative emotion that might plague this pivotal event in the life of the family. His compassion for his wife, whose body goes through so many profound changes over the nine months of gestation and the six weeks following birth, is infinitely greater than that of an observer or outsider who has forgotten that he, too, is the giver of life.

REBALANCING THE ROLES WITHIN THE FAMILY

It is a magnificent adventure to try on all the roles within the family unit so that you have a familiarity with each from the level of the heart. As you explore the elements of mother, father, and child within you, it is easier to adjust the channel of relation you have with anyone else in your family to be what you really want it to be. Only when you can intimately identify with the experience of another can you truly know them or be able to find a frequency of communication that brings you together.

This rebalancing and remeasuring of energy between the yin and the yang is going on around the planet. It is a part of the purpose of the difficulty in present relationships. You must begin to identify the male and female within you rather than in the mirror of another. The mirror projection is a slow process of growth for the soul because it may take lifetimes for you to recognize that you are just using the other to learn about yourself.

I have been astounded to witness that even in traditional societies some form of divorce or separation is becoming common. Divorce has a powerful effect on the family structure, especially on the children. In most societies the children are left with the mother rather than the father, although as fathers begin accessing the female within them, they are expressing more desire to raise the children themselves or be more participative.

These experiences are forcing individuals to discover and use the energies of the polarity within the self. The child separated from the father is forced to find the father within. This accesses male energy in a totally different way, as the child is catapulted into the consciousness of yang emotions, physical activity, and mental concepts.

As fathers come together with their children in concentrated blocks of time, such as weekend custody, they must play the mother, father, friend, and teacher. This allows them to open their repertoire of Inner Entities so they can express their inner feelings with the children. Imagine that suddenly you have a whole day with a child you once saw only mornings or nighttime. You have to find some way to communicate, whereas before you may have lived in the same household without really ever knowing each other. The child or the mother may have taken over some of the masculine or fathering roles in the home. The children are therefore no longer so dependent on you to fulfill their needs on those levels, but rather begin to connect with you on more universal levels.

As each member of the family dissolves the boundaries of his or her familial role, the communion between all is accelerated and heightened. Using the tools of the Inner Entities, each has a way of enhancing the attributes of yin and yang to form a new, highly functional personality within a group structure. For example, if you need to be more assertive or express something in a more visible way, you could ask the Inner Male to come forward and give you a color or a gift that will facilitate your yang expression. It only takes a second to visualize the Inner Male, and when you receive the gift or color that will help you feel stronger, you are setting in motion an energy that causes the body actually to alter its stance. You can feel that strong sense about yourself immediately. It is thrilling to discover that you can communicate and accomplish things you never dreamed you could, simply by using these latent energies within you. When the body has the opportunity to experience these essence energies, it triggers changes in the biochemistry, even in the glandular secretions that soften or amplify those characteristics that we consider to be female or male.

If you experience a lifetime in which you are the male and you are penetrating in a sexual way or protecting the family, or doing something mental, it will imprint your subconscious so that you feel comfortable with the same form of expression now. This is why you may be a tiny, frail female who loves to do very assertive or physical things. Your body remembers how to move in those old ways.

The personality is also affected by the memory of different

yin/yang expression. It is an illusion that the personality remains the same throughout all the myriad lifetimes: it does not. Our ego self is different in each life experience, for it is the actor upon the stage, and each role affords it an opportunity to become aware of the hologram.

As you begin working with the male and female in you, the Inner Father or Mother, the force of your divine wisdom can find more amplified expression in your life. It is a wonderful tool if you are experiencing transition in your life, moving in or out of relationships, jobs, or places. The variation of personality type, body, or theme reminds you that you are safe because you really have so many resources upon which to draw. You can therefore risk making new choices as you discard old unusable habits.

Working with the Inner Entities will open you to the nuances that express the energetics related to your familial experience. The form or feeling you perceive as representative of any specific one will holographically show you exactly where you are in terms of that yin/yang energetic in this moment. In other words, you will very much recognize yourself in the style or role of one or more of the Inner Entities as you play them out in everyday relationships. Communicating with them releases the "stuckness" of holding some emotional positionality toward male or female expression.

The Higher Self is absolutely brilliant in its choice of graphic representation of these energies in a way that you will be able to relate to them. The images that appear, and the subsequent messages or impressions that are related, always seem clear to the person receiving them. This is like picking a food off the shelf. If you feel that one of your essences can help you at any moment in your life, or you know that there is an imbalance, you can simply take a moment to call that energy into your consciousness. You can use its energy or allow it to speak to you so that you can deepen your self-knowledge.

Let me give you some examples that illustrate how these messages are given through the images of the Inner Entities, as people experience them in meditation.

INNER FATHER: twenty-six-year-old woman

He appears as a bloated, sloppy man from the Middle Ages in velvet, drooling grease down his chin while stuffing a chicken leg into his mouth. He takes everything within his reach and devours it—women, riches, everything. He has wives and children whom he never visits except to misuse.

Message: "This is your own memory; you were this miserable being. Your judgment of that experience caused you to choose a father in this lifetime who was removed from you, both physically and emotionally. You still carry that disdain—you cannot be told anything by your present father and feel he has nothing to offer you. Release me from that bondage and you will be able to give your wisdom to those around you now."

Comment: This person has been holding great unexpressed anger toward her father. Though she worked as a counselor for a few years, she is now involved in trying somehow to make up for something she feels she missed.

INNER MOTHER: six-year-old boy

She appears as a dark red sea with waves—energetic, but not scary or angry.

Message: Fairies playing in a humongous tree. "Have fun," Inner Mother says.

Fairies ask the question, "How was the sea made?" Inner Mother answers, "It was made by hot lava."

After this exchange, the Inner Mother enters the boy's energetic body through the eyes.

Comment: The Inner Mother is connected with this little boy's raw creativity, as represented by the primordial hot lava. He needs to be given the freedom to explore that force as a part of his play that will yield a strong creative talent.

INNER MALE: forty-seven-year-old woman writer

He appears as an Oriental-looking woman with a white kimono whose energy is spinning up around her body and out the top of her head, where it continues to spiral upward.

She gives a gift of a fan with which to "fan life; to fan the heart and upper chakras." The fan enters the body through the mouth and nose. (She feels this energy intensely and begins to vibrate and breathe in a fanlike fashion.)

Message: "You know all you need to know." She receives a

picture of a book with white pages. The top right corner is folded backward, making many pages.

Comment: This woman has been suffering "writer's block." She goes home and finishes the book, which she later sends to me. It is filled with profound knowing.

INNER MALE: fifty-three-year-old woman
   He appears as a Viking male, large and robust with one hand in the air. He has the energy of an adventurer. He is laughing, full of spirit, and his blue eyes sparkle. I feel energized just being with him. He touches my right chest in a playful yet sexual way.
   Message: He draws his sword and puts a headpiece on his head. He starts cutting something in cross sections. "Don't waste yourself on the frayed edges, go straight for the heart of the good stuff." He bursts into a golden comet rising from bottom left to upper right of my vision. I feel fantastically strong!
   Comment: This woman is very successful in many different projects, but she is still a bit timid about releasing her powerful energy. The Inner Male is encouraging her to let the adventurer take over and help her let go of her restraint. The vitality he exhibits will increase her own physical image of herself as a superhuman.

INNER CHILD: young man
   He appears as an unborn baby in the womb. Amber and golden pink light. He takes my hand, and I feel him walking through my arm. He asks for a neon blue pyramid. The child now looks like an oval mask with large white tubes for eyes. He gives me the gift of Truth, represented by a ladle with a slender handle and a disk on the end of it. It goes into my heart and has a quality of smoke or incense, which is very relaxing.
   Message: An image of a big iguana, who looks at me with a very serious expression. He says to me, "Take your power seriously. You must forgive yourself for what you've done." The residue of my guilt is held in the neck. The disk dissolves it. His eyes are wide open, and he comes into my body and I feel a warmth all over.
   Comment: This connection with the Inner Child is very important for the growth of the young man, as he has not yet begun to use his powerful spiritual knowing. He could easily have gone into a memory of another lifetime that is influencing him now, as represented by the pyramid and the mask of the child. The forgiveness will break loose the withholding of his power, as his Inner Child has now been birthed.

Connecting with your Inner Entities gives you a feeling handle on what is going on with you at any moment. It takes the frustration of vague, inexplicable feelings and puts them in a visual context to which you can relate. This creates a helpful energetic that can change the mood or situation entrapping you.

Contemplate how you experience each of these energies in you. If you can come to recognize them and their influence on your life, you will be able consciously to manifest your dreams and goals through the powerful application of their specific gifts.

APPLICATION
AND ILLUMINATION

To apply and illumine the feminine levels of consciousness in our daily lives, we must draw the formless (knowing) into interface with the manifest (doing) so that the yin and the yang can embrace and merge. At this intersecting point, energy erupts from its pure essence of knowing and is infused with matter, with thought and intention, so that it is sculpted into a form that is recognizable. That form is the way we live our lives. If the intuitive essence is active, we seem to be more successful in our endeavors because we have a better feel about what is happening and about the probable course of events. This gives us a gigantic edge on others in arenas of competition such as business and school and even in diverse fields like environment and international relationships. The feminine energy can be applied to our lives in specific ways. Whether we need answers in the boardroom, classroom, or living room, the capacity to turn to inner knowing can make the difference in the way we function on a daily basis.

Consciousness, then, is applicable to every millisecond of our lives, our survival, our future, and even our past. The powerful person simply holds the energy long enough to perceive all the choices that are available through that particular hologram.

If each time we came across a new situation we allowed ourselves to expand our focus to embrace all possible ramifications, to see the whole instead of just the individual parts, we would comprehend it at its core. Only through such comprehension can we transmute errors of shortsightedness. The challenge is the capacity to hold the focus of the entire spectrum so that we enter into dialogue with the laws of cause and effect. Otherwise, we are simply frictioning forces rubbing against each other because we can't gain a big enough perspective to discover the solution.

INTEGRATION

Most of us lead fractionalized lives in which we play a variety of roles that sometimes include the expression of entirely different personality types. For example, the "henpecked" husband may become the office tyrant, or the submissive secretary may return home and order her children around like a maddened drill sergeant.

The complexity of our lives forces us to struggle with the dilemma of integration—gathering up the extraneous ends of our forays into the world and tying them together. Integration seems like an impossible quest for most of us, and instead of attempting it, we compartmentalize ourselves with exterior activities and inner nuances, almost as if we were entirely different people in each role. We have a public persona and an inner, secret self who act and think very differently. Too often the face smiles and the mind thinks negative thoughts about other people and situations.

We tend to fit others into categories related to our fixed realities: there are those who belong to our personal life and others who are connected with our professional masks. In social situations, if we try to intermix people outside of their fixed settings, we usually encounter a disaster. This happens so often at parties where work colleagues and neighborhood friends come together to celebrate someone and find it difficult to relate to each other, causing stiffness and a sense of boredom or embarrassment. One reality is our identity in the yang world—in business or work outside the home—and the next reality is our relationships at home. Somehow we must find a point of reference that can transcend both worlds and dissolve the separation.

The only point at which all worlds meet, and from which they all come, is the spiritual sense of our soul. If we could get to the true self, we could translate this profound soul energy outward to hold as a constant of our being in any given situation. Using the soul as the center of our being or hologram, we could feel safe because we would be eternally the same—alone, in public, in mind, and in heart.

It is that old frustration when we burn all our energy in one role and then find we have nothing left to contribute to the others. This is the classic case of the person who works all day and returns to the home, where the family waits expectantly for some intimate, caring exchange. It never comes because the person's emotions have been spent on bosses, co-workers, and strangers who have triggered his or her competitive, survival energies all day long.

People who live three lives—the mother, career woman, wife; the father, executive, husband—must sandwich together a wide diversity of outside demands in order to keep pace with a loudly ticking internal time clock, squeezing time constantly until it feels as if there is none to spare. You can integrate these lives when the Emotional Body lets go of the need to survive. If you are willing to risk because you recognize that each experience is an opportunity for heightened consciousness, there is no gain or loss, win or lose, there is only the constantly expanding awareness of how the holographic puzzle fits together. By recognizing that this process is simply that of cause and effect, you can begin to create the fusion of purpose that manifests what you are looking to manifest.

If you are living your true self, from the center of your multidimensional hologram, you can hold several thoughts in different arenas at the same time. It is important to consciously command your brain to bring to your awareness any incoming

information that is useful and correlates wit'
are solving. Information from wide sectors
can be synthesized to bring meaning and c
is the famous think tank technique used by
educational institutions. The only differenc.. ..
putting together the scientist, the sociologist, and the econoᵐᵘˢᵗ,
you are incorporating all those perspectives as they live within
you! It is really exciting to scan the hologram and realize that
you can perceive from many different angles.

The trick is to realize that you can think about and attend to
several things at once without becoming confused. It is a wonderful opportunity to use the whole brain synchronistically.
Here's how.

Begin the day with a rundown of what needs to be accomplished in your various life arenas. Then ask your Higher Self
to take form. When you perceive this energy, ask the Higher
Self to shed its light on your mental list of activities. Visualize
them surrounded in light and then bring the image of your
Higher Self into your body. Now, feeling charged with this
wonderful energy, begin your meditation, allowing yourself
to be fed by this all encompassing energy before you have to
go out and give energy to the rest of the world. Just the
consciousness that you are being fed energetically helps tremendously to face the day. The Higher Self will order the
events synergistically so that solutions, ideas, and happenings
will occur at the perfect time sequence and your effectiveness
will triple.

As you keep your psychic channels open, you will also receive
data that may be related to emotional imagery or people and
places. These inputs require some response from you. As you
learn to send energy, you will feel more accomplished in your
life because you will gain a sense that you have worth and purpose
spilling forth from the experience of yourself as the channel of
energy.

ᴇ TIME TRAP

We are multidimensional beings, and the mind does very well on synchronous octaves if we teach it not to worry; instead, train it to perceive beyond the limitation of categorization rather than within the confinement of organization, teach it the skill of orchestration. The feminine energy is very good at orchestration and timing—everything goes on in concert, synergistically. If we use the feminine energy and live it all simultaneously, we do not get caught in the time trap.

Time becomes a trap when you try to compartmentalize reality into consecutive segments. These segments have less and less energy, and ultimately you have no energy and no time, either. Most of your time constraints are self-imposed because you are looking down the line to activities in the future and draining the potential of the moment.

If you use time multidimensionally, you have all the time in the world. While you are sleeping, for example, your expanded consciousness can gather all the particulates, all the increments of information and knowing you need and put them together for you, so that you wake up in the morning and say, "I got it. This is what I am going to do." Sleep time is the best for this because the consciousness is unencumbered by the doubting mind. Integration is easy within the scope of extended consciousness.

Both the traditions of the Kahuna and Silva Mind Control have demonstrated how to expand the time funnel by commanding the mind to find the answers, even while you turn your attention elsewhere. In fact, once you have set your intention, you must let go of the goal so that your Higher Mind can transverse the universal ethers to gather the appropriate energy and return it to you. You must release the goal to the forces that be, in order to start unfurling the process. As you allow the mind to expand holographically, it will solve your problems for you. This is the way of the feminine energy. If you use your consciousness to say, "When I wake up tomorrow morning, I am going to have the answer; I feel the solution to this problem coming to me," that is exactly what the mind will do. It will not only run through its data bank, but while you are sleeping, it will stretch out and pluck the answers from the other side of the veil!

Much of the difference between success and failure lies in this artistry of timing. Do not let the outside world dictate timing, but rather use the inner self to set the pace. All facets of your energy network are connected with a diverse matrix of subtle indicators that coincide with the synergetic moment for manifestation. There is an instinctual knack to seizing that moment to your advantage. You can become aware of your capacity to "sense" the moment when the energy is right to accomplish something. If it is not right, it will take you twice as long because of the proverbial "swimming upstream." You have to use multifaceted energy so that you are never locked into someone else's time frame. For example, let's say you are making a video. You have a program. It has to go on TV at a certain time. If your mind says, "I have to do this frame and this frame in order for it to be produced," you are always going to be panting. If, instead, you see the whole of it and ask your Higher Self to help you orchestrate it, you will see that you don't have to do it sequentially. It has nothing to do with trust. It does not happen in the mind. It happens in the living.

That simultaneous synchronistic kind of energy does not come from planning. It comes from magnetizing energy. You magnetize it, someone else might have missed that particular window of opportunity, but you cannot because it is yours. It is your destiny to produce that program. If you are having trouble getting hold of someone over here to make it happen, you go over there and do it around the other side. What happens is that it just congeals. This capacity to take all the little pieces and know that they will fuse together at the right moment is called *critical mass*. You simply pay attention to all the particulates, and just like the fairy godmother, as you touch this one and that one, you find that pretty soon there are so many that they start associating together and enter into critical mass; the fusion takes place. That is how manifestation happens.

Timing is the dance partner of the successful person. Knowing is always beyond the limitation of time itself. You have a powerful tool when you become aware that there is a timing to all things, that there is an energy that builds into critical mass, and that to rush out in that yang way before the moment is ready creates so much resistance that the goal is not accomplished. If, instead, you palpate each *particulate* energy until it reaches critical mass and then move it to the fore, you can reach the goal without resistance or strain.

Timing is a part of the feminine energy; it is the recognition of synchronicity. It can happen only if you sit within the self and ask, "Is this mine to do—now?" and then call forth the brilliance that you have to problem-solve, to bring it there.

PARENTING

Parenting is the perfect arena for practicing feminine capacities. Both men and women have the opportunity to hone their skills of nurturing and intuitive knowing with their children. It is so difficult to spend time with our children in today's world, yet we have the advanced techniques of psychic communication to help us bridge the absence of physical presence and help our children experience our love.

One of the great dilemmas for parents in today's world is the lack of prime time they have to spend with their children. Babies and toddlers enter the gates of child-care centers, never to return to the timeless attention of their parents. One look at the dis- connected youth of today gives us pause to reflect if this is a good idea, even though it is couched in the rationality of necessity. Great uneasiness and guilt are heaped upon us all as we wrestle with a possible solution to this problem. The result is that we spend too much energy worrying about our displaced children, and then when we are reunited at night, we have no energy to share with them, or they with us!

Unfortunately, children and spouses do not benefit from

worry, and I assure you that they perceive psychically all the confusion and guilt that fill up your inner connecting links. They are seeking the assurance and support that can come only through your clear intention and energetic transmission. This consciousness is the antithesis of that of the "worrier" who is always fussing about what others are doing. Worrying never helps the one who needs help, and it seriously drains energy. Underlying the concern is always subconscious guilt: guilt that we should do something, that we are responsible, or that any mishaps are our fault. This is partly because we carry so many negative thoughts and feelings around with us that haunt our minds, fearing that they will actually come true. We are petrified that others will blame us.

We need to cut the cord of external reproach and teach ourselves to lend love and good energy instead of negative anxieties. This is only a matter of training the consciousness to speak the language of universal symbolism. When you send a color, for example, you are not waiting for someone else to give approval or succumbing to the inundation of emotional discourses on who deserves what; rather, you are giving loving energy, which always makes you feel good.

Long ago, when I struggled with the solution to work versus home, my Higher Self taught me the principle, "Less is more." I was shown that it is not how much the mother is with the child or the woman is with the man. It is the way that they connect with each other. In other words, "Less is more" means that you can be away from your child physically, but if you send energy to the child, the child will always feel your presence because the psychic connection is never broken, so there is no loss.

My baby-sitters have always marveled that even my very young babies rarely cried for me while I was working, though they were still nursing. My secret is that I continually sent them energy while I was at work. Sometimes I psychically sent my smell or warmth, so that as they slept they felt me with them. I could always feel when they were looking for the breast, so I would send them psychic associations of the breast while they were

sleeping. I simply used the connection that they were familiar
with by being close to me. People often say that they feel my
presence close to them, and I actually am close, because my
loving consciousness is with them.

In truth, we are all connected by the psychic and karmic
network of relationship, whether we are aware of it or not. If you
find yourself thinking about someone, just ask them in your mind
what color they need and send it to them. Once you've sent them
energy, you are released to continue on, and they will feel that
they have what they need from you.

This is a great gift that can apply to any and all relationships.
Perhaps it will be a while before we learn to restructure the content
of our hours away from the daily nine-hour sludge, but we can
immediately transform the quality of those time capsules by re-
vamping our holographic attention.

Children all over the world return to empty houses every
afternoon after school. This is the opportune time for a five-
minute phone call to share their day, before the TV claims them
and they slip into the clutches of inertia. The psychic phone call
is happily received as well. You can play a game with your
children by asking them to guess what color you send them each
afternoon. The game reminds them that you care about them
and actually serves to strengthen the deep connections between
you.

Even more wonderful is to give them a chance to send you
color. Children witness your unhappiness and frustration but
have no avenue to help or heal you. When you let your children
know that you are willing to receive something from them, they
feel powerful and happy. They want to be of help, and they are
thinking of you. If, by keeping in touch psychically, you teach
your child not to worry about where you are or what is going
on, you will be taking a giant step toward creating a new generation of centered adults. Children are excellent healers because
their energy is boundless and it is natural for them to give. When
they learn at an early age to focus on others in this way, they are

able to perceive from levels of compassion rather than from emotional survival.

You need never worry about someone with whom you have this kind of rapport. If anything is wrong, you'll know it instantly. Having all your psychic connections covered helps you to keep your attention riveted on the job at hand so that you are much more successful—negative fears do not create interference.

Children today face the challenge of playing father and mother to themselves. Is it any wonder that they seem to be growing up so fast? On the other hand, if you communicate to them that the more they can do for themselves, the happier they will be, they can move toward feelings of pride about their independence rather than feeling an unquenchable longing for the parent who is never there. If they interpret your absence as abandonment, they will definitely play that out in every subsequent relationship, just as you have done. If you teach your children to be in touch with their Inner Parent, there will be much less projection and a lot more real communion between you.

Ultimately, parenting is less about having someone else fulfill all our needs than it is about the human themes of companionship, fusion, and oneness. As we explore our relationships with our children from the spiritual perspective of the soul, we amplify the ways we can come together and facilitate our mutual journey back to the source.

One of the greatest holes in our relationships with our children is our failure to demonstrate honesty. Children witness our lack of integrity and begin to practice it themselves as they grow older. Often they engage in activities they know are not good for them, indulging themselves for the sake of rebellion or group pressure. If you teach your children to listen to their inner voice, their Higher Self, the entire scope of discipline is opened up. For example, when your teenager wants to go out someplace and you suspect it will lead to trouble, if you say no, they will resist you and feel that you are oppressing or punishing them. On the other hand, when the young person asks the Higher Self about going out, they have a sense of self-destiny and responsibility to their own truth. Very often the Higher Self will be more conservative than you or I would ever dream of being!

We are weaning our children, in every sense of the word, much earlier today. Our error is that we push them into the outside world, thinking we are giving them a head start, rather than strengthening their inner world so that they can withstand the inevitable blast of external chaos. We don't seem to make the shift from being the primary caretakers to more amplified relationship roles with our children. Our connection becomes stunted after we no longer have to pick them up or feed them physically. We go from the body levels of physical caretaking straight to the mind, without the most important transitional thread of the soul. Yes, our heart is there, but we express our love through the haze of the material and mental planes. Our conversation with them revolves around what they think or what they do. Rarely do we share inner feelings or spiritual experiences and insights. Have you ever told your child about any intuitive or spiritual experiences you have had? Without confirmation from you that these levels are a part of life, you are sentencing your children to an empty life of spiritual isolation.

As our children grow older, we even become intimidated by them. Too many parents are actually uncomfortable around their teenagers and so use the schools as a buffer zone, placing the responsibility of relationship upon the teachers. Those with whom we spend so many hours of the day certainly become the prime objects of attention, much more than the ones we return home to at night and with whom we mostly share only a hurried meal and the TV.

Though most people are aware of television's detrimental side effects on the psyche, the lure of such a passive, effortless existence is irresistible when the need to escape from the pressures of daily existence is so great. Thus, we enter into mutual contracts whereby we subtly agree to leave each other alone so that we do not have to extend any energy to anyone else.

. . .

It is a tragic error for parents and educational institutions to depend on media presentation as a tool of learning simply because everyone engages in it. In the main, this is done not to inspire, but rather to escape. Passive awareness will never bring us to greatness. We must be able to go beyond the gathering of information, on to integrating it and then to the alchemy of creating something new. This is the octave of genius.

On the one hand, the capacity to be informed about world events may help us to acknowledge ourselves as citizens of the planet. On the other, the visual effect of witnessing the fear and the fury is drastically damaging to the psyche. As these images are laid down in the subconscious, they pollute our inner clarity so that the Emotional Body feels it must interfere because it is always so terrified. One of the major causes of sleep disturbance is the necessity to release all the negative imprints held in the body through emotional reaction. Today whole families sit through horror movies and newsreels without a flicker and yet experience great emotional upheaval without ever realizing that there is a connection.

Have you ever sat down and watched cartoons with your children? Perhaps you laughed as Woody Woodpecker or Bugs Bunny were slammed into some blockade by their "honorable opponent." Although you may excuse this as a harmless way to acknowledge aggression, it sets up a pattern of self-righteousness about aggression because this behavior is viewed as an acceptable response to something or someone outside the self. The cartoons considered the most exciting are the ones in which the bad guys are always trying to get the innocent kids. These are not appropriate messages for children or anybody else because they reinforce the Emotional Body's game of survival.

Even children know how to rationalize violence with the facade of "pretend." As long as we are not actually doing it, it is okay. The truth is that violence is the same whether it is verbal, emotional, or physical. If the intent is to use force, pretending and doing amount to about the same thing energetically. It's just that if we are pretending, we don't get into trouble. Yet both pretending and doing stem from the same feeling. Although it is important to have an avenue of expression for negative emotions, it must be balanced with the communication of loving feelings as well. If you could watch your children emulating life through their games, you would realize how heavily weighted they are on the negative. Our children do not play happiness and sharing games because they do not see us playing them!

Children act out what adults fantasize or hold symbolically. I'll never forget the first time my three-year-old son saw television. Witnessing a western shoot-out, he turned to me and said with chilling finality, "Men use guns." My explanation of time lapse and the Old West did not faze him. From that time on he was incessant in his desire to have a gun of any kind. Later that year, while we were in the village home of a friend in the Soviet Union, he discovered an old gun she had hanging on her wall. He begged her to show it to him, and when she allowed him to play with it, he ran around the room shooting at everyone. She shook her head in amazement and, even on my next trip to Russia, still commented upon his "violence." I was fascinated by the veils of the mind. For her, the gun's sinister effect was safely neutralized because it was only an artifact hung upon the wall. There her mind stopped because she knew she would not act out its true purpose. It was almost as if she had disassociated its intent from its form. But for the child, form and intent were one and the same. He was mystified by her disapproval since he was only pretending what he assumed she approved of because she had displayed it on the wall!

There have been too many prophecies by the major religions of the world telling us that these will be the times of war, hunger, and destruction. Whether in our modern sophistication we perceive these prophecies to be just "stories" is irrelevant because our great-grandparents believed them, so they are stored within our genetic imprints. We always manifest our prophecies! This is why so many people stoically observe the world events as if they were watching what they somehow expected to see. In fact, they are!

We need to realize that it is our collective consciousness that sculpts the future. We can affect the future by recognizing the underlying source of conflict and removing it. We must teach our children to perceive life as a hologram so that they can consciously alter what they have inherited, on all levels. They must learn that when there is a threat, it cannot be averted by fear, aggression, or denial. It must be met with wisdom and energy that can unravel the congestion and open up the options for response and action.

EDUCATION

Recognition of the value of intuitive knowing and holographic problem-solving could bring education up to a whole new revolutionary level of application. Linear thought and emphasis on logic have placed us too far on one side of the human equation to ensure happy, well-balanced individuals. As a result, students are turning away from school or are facing life with no meaningful preparation to cope with its demands. Overload seems to be the order of the day, and even teachers have begun to look for a means of shedding the burden of an overwhelming amount of information that is expected to be stuffed into the cognitive mind.

I have begun the Nizhoni School for Global Consciousness to train a new kind of awareness in children of all ages. Undaunted by age or national or familial background, these young people set out on a most magnificent journey to find a niche in the world. They study themselves through the multiple layers of personal psyche and higher consciousness, as well as through the body of humanity, the planet, and the galaxy. They study the intersecting spin points between all things living, dreamed, or designed. They are taught techniques for the coalescence and volition of energy and matter.

One of the ways we make the study of energy concrete is to get them involved in the energies of nature. They have developed the skill of calling the rain and are successful at doing this from a distance, so that we monitor our intention to bring rain to someplace and then witness the result. When they experience that their conscious intention has produced a verifiable result, they understand the power of consciousness from a new perspective and also have a sense of value within the universe.

While Nizhonis may study the facts necessary to master any discipline, they learn how to learn through their inner guidance. We teach them to scan the *Higher Mind* for clues and ideas that help them see the relevance of what they are learning and explore new ways of putting it to use. One concept I use a lot is the idea that we teach what we learn. To this end, they will study a subject and then give a workshop in which they teach it to others. This ensures not only that they learn the material, but that they are challenged to find meaning and application in it. Nizhoni gives workshops on such widely divergent topics as environment, inner peace, parent/child relationships, advanced learning techniques, sense of success, and sense of the earth.

In the past, all the higher octaves of knowing were kept under the shrouds of mystery and secret energies. Today, without embarrassment, we can apply knowing in very practical terms to our daily lives. Intuitive and spiritual understanding make a huge difference in the way we live our lives. It is imperative to take this yin energy out from under the mystery and into the mundane.

The crucial key to this transformation lies in your willingness to be visible and overt with your capacities, because it is visibility that allows these abilities to be applied. The great personages of the world, whether they were applying their wisdom on spiritual, educational, or business levels, have always used what they accrued in so many lifetimes to enhance their capacity to access energy and knowing well beyond the limitation of the linear mind. In their own way they tried to tell us the source of their genius, even though we could not hear them; witness Einstein and his mathematical dream fields!

In a world of such complexity, providing proof of knowing is analogous to honor and truth. I remember my abject agony in seventh grade as I looked into the incredulous eyes of my algebra teacher and tried to explain that there was a way the symbols on each side of the equation matched up by themselves, but I couldn't show him how I did it so instantaneously. I just "saw" the answers. He knew I wasn't cheating, but neither of us could explain what was going on. Instead of encouraging me, he chose to close his mind to the unfathomable, and with one suspicious pronouncement he crushed forever my delight in the magic of equation. Without a format for explanation, I was doomed to shame, and a bright star on the mathematical horizon slipped irrevocably from the sky!

There can be no true education that does not encompass source. All science today is based on the penetration of the invisible worlds, and yet it holds itself separate from spiritual essence. It is a tragically stiff and forced separation because science, which begins from the yang energetic, must ultimately reach toward and acknowledge the God source, which is yin, as the fountain of all knowing and bring it forward to be used by all.

We are very close to merging these two poles because once the veil to the unknown is pierced, we have entered inextricably into the realm of Divine Source, which we must embrace with all our faculties. The farther into the universe we seek, the more our consciousness receives spiritual understanding. Isn't it interesting to observe the metamorphosis of the astronauts as they go forth with their minds to probe the galaxy and return with the radiance of profound realization!

If, within the educational field, we could recognize that piercing the veil allows us to gather source information without having to understand it intellectually, simply by harvesting it from the unmanifest, we would enrich the excitement of learning.

We do not have to reduce everything to the confines of the linear. First we must allow the Higher Mind to scan from the awakening pulse of alpha and theta brain waves relevant and raw information that can be synthesized into an integral whole of something new. These brain frequencies are the octaves of dreaming and creative thought. They encompass what some call the function of the right brain, or what I call the *feminine energy*. The capacity to bring together particulates, or increments of knowing, to create new wisdom and understanding is the function of learning. Science is the stabilizing glue that allows it to endure and become a part of our world. The progression is first to become aware of something that is real and then to allow it to teach us. This is the true nature of science: as we witness it, as we observe it, we learn.

The power of feminine fusion is that capacity to include, to take in, and to process experience. Experience is the only truth, the only teacher. When you say, "How can I use this new energy in my daily life?" you have to be able to feel when you have switched on the feminine energy, the spiritual funnel. Feeling the guidance of inner knowing helps so much to reduce the fear of not being right, not being able to explain, or not being intelligent enough to learn what you seek.

Thought creates matter. The reason we are frustrated and limited in our lives is that we do not get beyond the thought. We only fantasize or contemplate when we actually need to bring the energy to life. We have to follow the thought energetically to its result, to feel the quality of what it creates. This is simply cause and effect again. Once you start creating something, you are accessing the energy, the pure energy. Then you can follow all the directions in which it moves, feeling it in your heart and in your pineal gland, in the ways that are called intuition or precognizance. All these things that you think are so mysterious are really just the natural flow. If you let go of the mind, the mind will automatically go out there to the reaches of Source.

The minute the mind expands, it will come across cosmic energy, and that is when you encounter all those experiential perceptions of heightened awareness that offer the genius level of potential, such as the inventor and the problem-solver. Intelligence is really a measure of the capacity to commune with all there is.

Genius-level awareness is a sensation inside the mind, inside the body, that becomes absorbed in knowing and thus dissolves the limited self without effort. You have the choice at every moment to focus either on the problem or on the solution. You must go back and awaken the Higher Mind, back to the levels of wonderment. The answer is inherent in every question. It is veiled from you only because of the illusion that you cannot expand enough to grasp it, that you can see only one facet at a time, which is certainly true of the linear mind. Yet you have tremendous faculties inherent in your human birthright; everyone has the potential to become a genius.

At the Nizhoni School for Global Consciousness, we teach students to embrace the requisite variety of life by thinking holographically and yet studying the interaction of all things. Virtually all their studies are brought back to personal relevance with *themselves in the center of the picture*, whether it is the vague familiarity of historical imprints, language, or mathematical equations for a cleaner environment.

For example, our three college-level schools interact to create a global perspective for problem-solving. The Academy of Ecology and Energy sets a priority theme for action. The Global Business School works closely with the Arts of Expression School to create packaging that will provide each student with a personal relationship through his or her own area of expertise, to then give something relevant to the world. Through their mutual cooperation they gain an understanding of the myriad pieces that fit together to make the whole.

Education today has faltered and is on the precipice of disaster. Our children either are not learning or are being squeezed into molds that ultimately cannot sustain our existence because they are not being taught to discover universal truth. This exploration is thwarted because teachers erroneously think that to teach something, they must have all the possible answers. These answers are not in textbooks. At Nizhoni we teach young people to "seek." The role of the teacher is as guide, not judge and examiner. The term *harvesting people* can have a good connotation as well as one of expedience. Nizhoni students learn to harvest the knowing of everyone we meet, because everyone has some pearl of wisdom he has gathered in life. The art of extracting that pearl is the subject of one of the classes I teach on communication. It begins with an attitude of searching for someone's innate knowing, not the holes in that person's presumptions.

Communication should be one of the core skills taught in any school. Communication has the requisite variety of modalities so crucial to success: how to merge the head and the heart; how to dissolve opposition; how to commune beyond the mind, the culture, the language.

How could we hope to graduate successful and useful individuals from institutions of learning that give absolutely no clue how to experience or explore life? Yet not only are we hesitant to teach children about human psyche, we are loath even to suggest that there might be mysteries inside them that are inexplicable and yet applicable to life's quests.

We must not flinch at the great questions of life because they inevitably lead us into spiritual discussions. Teachers are afraid to speak of the deeper questions, lest parents point a finger at them for entering into the dangerous terrain of religion. They need not be so afraid. You can house something that is totally nontraditional in traditional terms. For example, in New Mexico the public school teacher is not allowed to do anything that could be construed as "meditation" or "visualization," but he or she can talk about the body. A teacher can say, "Ask your body where it is holding fear." The teacher is doing something that triggers visualization and meditation, but it is done in a way that does not threaten anyone.

The Nizhoni School for Global Consciousness is very successful academically partly because we have many specific techniques for increasing the learning edge. One of them has to do with reducing fear, a major concern in the learning process. The fear of failure or embarrassment becomes an ongoing anxiety early in the life of the child. So when we begin at Nizhoni, we first clear the residue of fear out of the body and set up conscious pathways to access information stored in the brain. As the fear recedes, the learning curve rises sharply.

Nizhoni offers short intensives for teachers to help them get rid of their own fears about seeking true knowledge. Instead of starting by bumping up against the limitation of what you can teach or express in the classroom, explore for yourself the outer spectrum of potential that is available when consciousness expands. Discomfort about such intimate topics is usually relative to the teacher's willingness to explore them personally. Yet such profound mysteries and contemplations can easily insinuate themselves into classroom discussions without being viewed as a threat. You could be teaching a class in grammar and solicit thought-provoking answers to questions such as "Who are you?" and "Why are you here?" These probes will transform students because the answers are not just words, but palpable radiations that set students on the path of wisdom.

If we must fall back on the old stale idea that our spiritual nature is limited to a religious positionality concerning the whims of God, then we could never survive its exploration in the classroom. But, instead, if we would trust our children to express Divine Essence in pure form, we could advance the expression of creative celebration for life, rather than imposing on them the killing field of archaic religious domination.

RELIGION

One of the areas most in need of feminine fusion is religion. Religion is the masculine form of spirituality. The translation of all that is divine into the laws and specified order set forth by groups of men has placed sacred life dangerously within the clutches of group paranoia and separatism. This is the yang force in its most isolated expression. Although religion expounds upon love and the merits of focusing on God, it lives like wild dogs scrapping for one piece of meat. As if only one can win God's favor and the rest should be exterminated, religion has embroiled itself in the futile ploy for territory that will never belong only to humans or to one tiny sector of the universe.

The world has grown too small to accommodate such narrow perspectives. All too often the pure lure of power and control is tucked neatly within the folds of religious righteousness. Mankind has indulged in too much interpretation of Divine Intent. As we have attempted to define the universe by defining what is holy and what is not, we have unleashed the fires of religious fanaticism, all because everyone wants to be acknowledged by God. What would happen, if instead of interpreting God to be a human just like us, with all our emotions, we could experience ourselves and God as infinite form and energy?

We have stylized God in rituals and mental concepts that give the trappings of intricate complexities, which serves only to keep the most profound experiences out of reach for us. Too many of our conversations about God are stifled in mental straitjackets or caught in endless mediation, bargaining over life and death.

The gifts of heaven, nirvana, supreme consciousness, and the void that are spoken of in religions around the world are only a very small portion of all that is available. Each religion has so much to offer in the expansion of our expression, devotion, and celebration of the Divine Source. At the Nizhoni School, we explore the almost infinite variety of these fascinating manifestations to enrich our vocabulary of the sacred because it is important to amplify our shared human gift of the divine, not to diminish it.

It is easy to crystallize awareness through the limitation of definition. Yet enlightenment goes far beyond the heights of spiritual goals, because as we aspire to "God" consciousness, the experience of God is pushed beyond the boundaries inherent in the moment. God grows through us. All the gods of our universe are seen by us as encapsulations of the material world that is never static, always unending. It is only the hungry Emotional Body that insists on limiting the relationship to the boundaries of *Homo sapiens*.

As you move into each new level of cosmic awareness, you open so that you receive more and more. You can bridge the gap between universal consciousness and humanity and between religion and spirituality by focusing on the translation of the divine into the third dimension.

For example, imagine that you are carrying the divine spark and that it moves through you into the world. Practice talking like God. In this way you are triggering your consciousness into a level of knowing that alters the energy in the body. The moment the Higher Mind dictates, "I am now talking like God; I am now practicing God," you are imprinting God in all of your being. You are developing a repertoire in which you continually create the divine thought that creates God anew. As you talk like God, God talks like you. This is the power of intention that actually changes the universe through you! It is very healing. Instead of the incessant reprimand that you are not good enough for God, as you include God, your whole life begins an upward spiral into the light. You lose your fear of expansion and reach to receive, and as you receive you begin to receive everything as God. The great Indian guru Baba Muktananda expressed it so beautifully: "See God in each other."

This is the way of the heart, the clearest truth. This is the feminine principle of inclusion: expansion through inclusion. It is urgent now that this feminine, yin energy be integrated into religious life. If the family of humanity could begin to see the bliss of sharing God, we would be able to transcend the grappling base of our present existence. As the feminine enters the structure of religion, religions will enjoy each other's gifts rather than destroy the bodies of those who would worship and expand the divine.

At the Light Institute we guide people to experience the divine energies directly without becoming entrenched in them as a personification. This allows us to move on to cosmic levels of consciousness, even beyond the realm of the human, and to see that the masculine and feminine energies are not separate but are really inside each other.

Not only is inclusion a major point of reference, but in that expansion to include comes a new kind of energy. It is the energy that belongs only to people who are whole and therefore have gained clarity and compassion; these are the energies of loving that are fully extended. All beings, men, women, and children, have as the central point and the core of their being lovingness.

When we use that kind of energy to create abundance around us, it can become effortless. As each being begins to make contact with the energies that allow for lovingness, each of us becomes the healer. The healer, the priest, the teacher, the protector: all of these are aspects of the self, calling out to be recognized and acknowledged.

BECOMING THE HEALER

One of the greatest opportunities to experience the transcending potential of the feminine principle is in the area of healing. Your own body is the best place to practice the art of spiritual connection. You are the most experienced expert on the mechanisms, habits, and necessities of your magnificent biological instrument.

Illness and disease come about as the result of blocked energy that causes a dysfunction in the body's otherwise inpenetrable system of defense. The trash that collects within the cells disrupts the electrical magnetic balance until even the electrons of the atoms become disoriented and are thus available to destructive energies circulating throughout the internal and external environments. The presence of germs, bacteria, and viruses is not a threat to an organism in a state of balance because it has an ample defense system.

When you feel ill, your body is telling you that there is a disruption in its energy field. It may be that the Emotional Body is out of balance because of the constant stress of having to answer its insatiable need to be reassured. Because the mind does not control the Emotional Body, you must alter this state of affairs through communication with the spiritual body. Thus, if you give yourself a moment of meditation, you can calm these inner anxieties so that your body will respond to a clear command to overcome the "evil chi," as Chinese medicine calls these invading energies.

The physical body, however, is very susceptible to commands from the mind body. Therefore, if you review the message your body is giving you when you don't feel well, you will be surprised how quickly you can recover when you tell the body that it is time to be well!

Simply bring your consciousness into the part of the body that is expressing pain or imbalance and ask what message the body is giving you. Then breathe deeply and empty your mind so that your body can speak. You'll be fascinated by the thoughts and insights that seem to come to you from your body. Use the color technique to synchronize with your body and return to balance by drawing a color into that area of the body. After practicing a while, you'll find that your body will respond almost immediately to your command.

There is a wonderful feeling of satisfaction that comes when you can motivate or alter the body. It makes you feel that you can play a part in your own destiny. Many people have great fears about their body. It is absolutely life changing to discover that one can protect oneself by being in touch internally with the body. This is preventive medicine in its pure and complete form. It must be taught to our children at an early age, so that they can develop a natural resistance to any intruding energies.

Today we have entered into a frightening battle with resistant strains of bacteria and viruses that have adapted their molecules to the ever-increasing strength of our antibiotics. The careless overuse of antibiotics has put us in jeopardy around the world as more virulent strains alter themselves faster than we can develop new forms of antibiotics. It is sending us the same message that reverberates in the other arenas of our life: "All that is powerful must come from within." The conscious body can overwhelm and discard negativity if it is instructed to do so.

If you can recognize that illness is neither permanent nor punishment, but, rather, a challenge to communicate with your body, which is processing your experiences as well as aiding the soul's lessons, you can take responsibility and become your own healer. Most of the great healers I have known have experienced terrible diseases and conquered them to begin their life's work of healing others.

All of us have the right and potential to greatly influence the health of others. We cannot make them well or take their diseases away from them, but we can lend healing energy that they can use to heal themselves. This is the feminine energy at work, and men can do it every bit as exquisitely as women. Perhaps that is a secret reason men become doctors: deep inside them is the desire to express their healing feminine force. Yet one of the discrepancies in Western medicine is the overemphasis on intellectual understanding and underemphasis on the intuitive, loving presence that is what truly heals.

You know how hard it is to concentrate once you are feeling pain. This is where the soothing, loving energy of another can help to focus the attention so that the body gets a clear mandate as to what to do to heal itself.

In a healing situation, you must command the higher frequency of energy so that it can lift up the other person. As you create an environment in which someone who is ill can look at

APPLICATION AND ILLUMINATION • 109

the purpose of the illness, they will begin to recognize that they are in a process, but that they are not the process themselves. As they receive the higher-octave energies you are making available, they will recognize themselves on these levels. This is the threshold of power. You will feel the awareness of two divine beings sharing energy.

You can do this for someone even from a distance. The crucial thing is to ask them, in a meditative state, to give permission to be helped. I do this by asking them what color they need to heal themselves. When I perceive the color, I begin to transmit it to them until I feel they are full.

I remember one woman whose father had been lingering with a fatal disease for many months. It caused the whole family untold grief to witness his slow suffering. The first time she asked him psychically what color he needed to be well, he asked for pink and gave her a glorious smile, which she had not seen him do for many months. She went to bed feeling that at last there was something she could do for him. In the early morning she was awakened by a call from the hospital to inform her that he had passed away peacefully in the night. At first she was worried that she had done something wrong. I explained that, on the contrary, her father only needed that pink color of love to help him know that he was finished and could now let go. His quiet passage was a great relief to the whole family.

What usually happens when someone becomes ill is that everyone around them is clutched by an uneasy sense of guilt. It is a feeling that we are somehow complicit in their illness through all our negativity. Deep within us we know that our thoughts and intentions toward them are sometimes filled with the shadow side of our being. Nowhere is there a child or an adult who has not wished someone gone, out of the way of their life, in at least one moment of impassioned rage. When something does happen to them, we are riddled with guilt because of our unspeakable feelings and thoughts. Somewhere in our being we also know that they know we are feeling these things, and we even wait to be punished. In fact, we sometimes feel angry at them for being sick, since we perceive the illness as their way of getting back at us. I call this the "tyranny of the weak," when one who is obviously weaker due to illness completely controls the decisions, conversations, and lives of others. Would that we could meet this situation with compassion instead of seething resentment with which so many people struggle in cases of prolonged disability.

We may begin a crisis situation with love and the earnest intention to support, but all too quickly that helping-hand energy dissipates as we become restless to return to our own endeavors. This lack of staying power comes from feeling that we only have a certain amount to give or that we only owe so much, as if loving care were a commodity rather than a karmic opportunity. The more negative our inner thoughts, the more resentment feeds the fire of our vicious circle.

If you send healing energy to someone, you are releasing and dissolving your indebtedness to them. It is so freeing to be the giver, and you can experience how people will let you go if you just give them the minute amount they are asking from you.

As you learn to send healing energy, you might be brave enough to suggest that all the members of the family replace their worrying with this active form of healing. It could become a magnificent bonding tool for families and friends who are all engaged in mutual focus on a loved one who is ill.

It is wonderful to practice healing energy as a group endeavor. When several people send healing energy simultaneously, the results are often extremely powerful. In my children's school, we witnessed goats with cysts be completely healed in two days as the children sent them energy!

As each person takes responsibility to become one's own healer, the entire orchestration or administration of healing energies on this planet will change totally. Rather than overcoming parasitic organisms, or battling negative viruses, we can instead place our attention on the source of life itself and therefore learn the lessons and the spiritual purpose for all imbalance.

We must move away from the technology of disease that is based upon the germ theory because it does not provide a scenario for healing in concert with our profound relationship to our own body. Healing potential comes from the power of the self to choose and the wisdom of the body to know. Healing could become a different kind of activity, an activity that everyone participates in, including children. As we use the feminine, spiritual recognition of all experience, we have the opportunity to change the future by teaching it to the future generations.

When a small child recognizes that bumping the knee is expressing something, that it is a message whispered especially to that child from the body, he can begin to listen to that message and alter the outcome by the way he moves in his body.

Rather than growing up being the victim of the physical body, he can allow healing to become part of the challenge, the initiation of life, the pleasure that sparks his attention and our power.

BUSINESS

Nowhere has the fusion of the feminine (the formless essence) and the masculine (the manifest) a more magnificent potential than in the arena of the business world. Here, all our personal pursuits run headlong into the competitive stream, where our instincts can carry us into the eddy of success or dash us against the rocks of greed by the thrust of power. The search for power has been a driving force of humanity for as long as we have sought to identify the self. As we lost our connection with the infinite, we felt more the fear of survival and the need to pretend supremacy, lest someone or something overpower us. This gave rise to the use of alchemy by which the goal justified the means. Anything or anyone was fair game to be used as an instrument of individual will or attainment.

In the Middle Ages, alchemy was used to shape things into whatever was expedient for the personal self. The alchemical process is the extension of the personal will to force matter into a purposeful form. Perhaps all of us have practiced alchemy at some point in the evolution of our souls, but we must now see the advantages of using our power in cooperation with others for the gain of us all. Manifestation today must be detached from selfish aims; instead it must allow all of the parts to fuse and come together without exclusive ownership.

In business today we have revolutionary opportunities to extend beyond the personal into levels of cooperation. The feminine arts, such as inclusion and cooperation, are finding their way into the global business arena. For example, one of the major trends is the merging of different companies and even whole economic communities. The economic climate of Eastern and Western Europe is one of fantastic excitement as a new form of symbiotic communion emerges.

The capacity to recognize that something can be shared or given up without the competition, without war, for the good of the whole, is exactly the lesson that is coming to us all.

Here is a classical example of how to use spiritual energy in life. When you meet with resistance, and you challenge it in the old masculine pattern of King of the Mountain, your choices are limited. It is either "You win" or "I win." If instead you use the feminine spiritual energy to go to the source of the resistance, you can overcome it. Perhaps it is a person—or persons—who blocks your accomplishments. Why do these people resist? They may be afraid. You must evaluate who is behind the economic machinery and acknowledge your karmic relationship with them. You can direct the energy that will help them to dissolve fear by showing them who you are and upholding them, for example. When they are free, they will let you pass, so to speak. You do not have to conquer them. You do not have to overwhelm them. You just have to lift them.

It is so easy to pretend that we are communicating through artificial intelligence, spreadsheets, or complicated corporate structures, but these are only the handmaidens of external human relationships and not the voyages of the soul seeking to extend its expression through fusion with other souls. We will never outgrow the teachings we give each other.

In a business boardroom, if you are arguing in order to take control, you are responsible for the resulting limitation of choices. But if instead you become aware of the energy potential carried by all those present, you can focus and orchestrate the energies in such a way that everyone can be "harvested" to contribute to a mutual manifestation. True leaders are those who encourage expression and creative responsibility in others: not in competition, but in cooperation. It is the power of the feminine energy to orchestrate situations and people so that they work together, creating a complementary energy for the good of the whole.

This is what is going on even in political arenas at the grassroots level around the world. People are suddenly realizing, "If you and I get together and we stand up and say, 'No,' we have a power we didn't know existed." Collective influence will happen more and more as individuals begin to access and awaken unlimited spiritual energy that gives power to the evolution of the way things are. They are the way they are so that we can experience what is necessary for growth. The most important revelation is to perceive that we are actually doing this together for our mutual growth! You and I can evolve with grace, rather than with struggle. Now, in this time of adversity, we must begin by recognizing each other and discovering how to combine our energies for manifestation. As we open to working collectively, we become much more attuned to our commonality and how it can work for us.

Europe is a fantastic example of the merits of karmic recognition. Western Europe is learning the multifaceted advantages of sharing, while Eastern Europe is discovering the power of collective consciousness to alter reality. It is a perfect resolution for old karmic lessons, as each helps the other to dissolve the past and embark upon a more ample future that is setting a model for the entire world.

It is fascinating to watch how whole nations move through the karmic threshold to emerge with an entirely different perspective. It is not history that teaches us. We all too often repeat and repeat history until the consciousness catches up on a spiritual level and swings around the spiraling hologram. Taking individual responsibility has to do with the power of choice. We have to trust the self. Since very few people trust themselves, we project onto everyone else that "you are not going to come through for me, so I cannot risk really committing to you." If only we could understand that any demise comes from inside and that anyone besides ourselves who is playing a leading role is doing so at our request! It is a challenge to practice the surrender of cooperation and have a sense of power at the same time. It is the feminine energy that illuminates the answer that comes from the level of the soul, reminding us that we are ultimately indestructible. We can afford to set something in motion and allow it to follow its own current.

Because business has the potential to demonstrate and design so many forms of relationship, it has a unique role to play in terms of the expression of the soul. As women enter the marketplace, men will be forced to develop their emotional skills of communication, as women often do business on the basis of their intuitive and emotional perceptions. It may be the drive of her Inner Male that directs a woman successfully into the business arena, but ultimately she will evaluate and make choices through the instincts of her Inner Female. So men who have strongly evolved Inner Females are much more likely to be successful co-partners.

The percentage of new businesses owned or run by women is skyrocketing. This fact in itself will force people to begin relating to each other from their inner being level rather than from stereotypical patterning. Then it may be the *man* who becomes aware of his tendency to use seduction as a tool for acceptance and security. He may find that his female boss is acutely aware of his pretense and thinks him less trustworthy and strong. This may force a deepening of his sense of himself and ultimately change the way he relates to the outside world.

This buying and selling in the sexual marketplace provides

immeasurable teaching tools for the Emotional Body to discover its glitches and illusions. The business world, like the body, will reflect and reveal the truth of your inner being. In other words, wherever you do not listen to the messages and cues coming to you from the physical world, because you want it to be different from what it is, you will ultimately pay the consequences for that denial. If you exhibit dishonesty or even expediency of action, you will bring the probable reality of experiencing the result of these things firsthand. It is simply the law of cause and effect.

However, you can use the feminine potential of knowing to precognate what might happen in any business situation. If you view the situation from the clarity of the laws of cause and effect, you will realize that what you set in motion will create a tendency or channel to an end result. For example, you can ask the Higher Self how to move in this direction or that direction, for the purpose of financial success as well as any other. The Higher Self has no preconclusions that abundance of any kind is outside the spiritual domain. In fact, it is an inevitable result of contact with universal realms. We simply have not learned how to use abundance as one of our rights. If we could discover the laws of energy that govern abundance, we would learn the lessons of grace. We struggle because we have forgotten our right to translate energy into any form: money, love, or even psychic awareness.

The ability to "know" or intuit is available to anyone who is willing to be receptive to the currents that turn the tide. This receptivity is something you can practice through meditation. Often the knowing that comes as a result will point out aspects of the situation that would never have occurred to you. The mind must be cleared so that probable realities can present themselves via energetic pathways.

For example, one of the major issues in any business is the optimal growth rate. You can effect the perfect stretch among source, supply, and expansion by *feeling* the relationship of each. Since there are so many variables, you must *sense* the growth. You can learn to feel the point of critical mass when the energy must create more of itself. Ask your Higher Self to show you what growth would look like. You will experience the answer holographically, perhaps visually or even through the sense of pressure. Simply open yourself to perceive it in meditation. If you push this too hard or try to do too much, you will experience the strain that is related to any growth. When you try to visualize something that doesn't want to happen, it is next to impossible to get it in focus. I call it "swimming upstream."

If you want to manifest something in business, the first question to ask is, "Is this appropriate for me?" If you get the answer "No," it is not because you are unworthy or could not accomplish it, but merely because it does not further your experience. Either there are not enough energies in play to bring it to critical mass, or circumstances of which you could not be aware would cause it to fail. It is crucial to perceive when this is taking place so that you can let it go and allow whatever shift needs to occur. You must clear your Emotional Body of useless attachment, or it will tend to cling to something that has little potential. However, you must also ferret out any silent imprints of limitation that would cause you to overlook solutions and then justify to yourself why you were unsuccessful.

When you have come to know your own Inner Female and Inner Male, you can direct them to the guidance of your life. Through your sensibilities, you can know if any situation necessitates the strength of the Inner Male or the attunement of the Inner Female. The orchestration of their energies can be a fantastic triumph over the Emotional Body, for the capacity to perceive in a detached yet open way carries with it a wonderful sense of self-destiny. Calling upon the frequencies of energy you have stored inside you can completely change the outcome of any endeavor.

In the work environment, there are those who need you to lead or show other masculine qualities, even if you are a female. Others may seek you out for your knowing or as a source of inspiration or support. Through the energies of your Inner Entities, you can access myriad responses that will help you to be successful with these co-workers.

As you are reviewing your success at communication with fellow co-workers, observe the various channels of relation you use with different people. If you see that your Inner Male is competing with another male energetically, you can immediately end the war by tuning that channel to the one of teacher or soul friend, for example. Perhaps you are playing father, with the result that people around you keep waiting for your permission or for you to do it. The game of the benevolent father is a common pitfall of CEOs. This will ultimately exhaust the creative energies, and it is so much more effective to create an environment in which each person is focused on the highest contribution to the group, rather than waiting for "Father," whom they will alternately respect and despise. These covert emotional energies can be very destructive to the accomplishment of any project and the CEO's ability to manifest, no matter what the business plan may be.

In these situations, you only need to lift your energies onto those octaves of spiritual knowing that facilitate the clarity to pursue what needs pursuing or to recognize when it is time to let go. You can say to your Higher Self, "How can this be transmuted?" By shifting onto the octave of problem-solving, you alter the level of influence. For example, the answer may be to send the person a color. What color does this person need to alter the frequency so that you can work together or attain a mutual goal?

If you find yourself locked in a verbal battle, send a color while you are discussing. The result is miraculous! Usually the other person will almost immediately change his voice level and attitude because he is so pleased to receive something from you. He may not be aware he is doing it, but he will instantly tune to psychic levels to perceive what is happening. Also, the moment you start to send a color, you have broken the emotional impasse caused by your refusal to yield. You will both discover that you can agree. The moment you ask the color needed by the person, you have committed yourself to removing the obstacles and releasing the karma that separates you. From this perspective, you cannot have a negative experience.

When you observe the laws of abundance and success that operate in the business world, you must acknowledge their relationship to your karma. This is not an esoteric statement, it is a practical statement. It means that if you begin to access the source in you that says, "I am learning the lesson of abundance," for example, you realize that you were born to have this experience because it is necessary for your growth. You must learn to use its power. It does not increase your value as a human being; it does, however, increase your opportunity to take responsibility for yourself and others.

There is far too much guilt and judgment about money in the world today. Those who do not have it begrudge those who do and yet seek desperately to have it, too. Money provides a lesson about the opportunity of abundance and how it relates to the use of power and creativity. There is a "sense" of money that can be used to attract it. We often joke that someone can "smell" money. This is absolutely true insofar as people have recordings of the feelings and sensations they associate with the money experience. Stop and think about this for a moment. What is your sense of it?

Successful businesspeople acknowledge that they use their intuitive force to give them insight and information. However, it takes great clarity to listen only to what belongs to you, rather than to argue for what your passion insists you must have. The tendency to greed disrupts the delicate balance of giving that is key to energy flows. If you are stuck on the taking cycle, you will ultimately build up a backwash of energy moving away from you that will cost you much more than a little compromise or generosity does at the outset.

If employers could tune in to the karmic choices of their employees about money, for example, they would be infinitely more successful in picking "winners." If someone in your office or firm has a subconscious imprint that he does not deserve abundance, that person will constantly sabotage the profit margin. You can learn to spot these energies by sensing beneath that person's veneer, deep into the Emotional Body, to discover what energics are actually lurking there. There are several kinds of energy patterns that cause problems: first, there is the person who is always doing battle with whatever is the goal. This person views a world in which everything is a personal encounter with the ego. He continually creates an impossible quest in which he is the good guy fighting insurmountable odds to conquer the enemy, who may be a client or even his own company. He enlists you in the saga of endless negotiating, which all too often ends in a valiant but unsuccessful attempt on his part. He struggles so hard that you are lulled into applauding his efforts rather than focusing on the cold fact that he didn't make it. This is the "Don Quixote," perpetually tilting at windmills. Around the world people are engulfed in this activity and are often viewed as the trusted, tireless, and faithful. With them, there is always a flurry of action, followed by the disclaimer.

A more dangerous variation of this is the gallant "victim," who repeatedly suffers the blows of treachery in one form or another. It is extremely important to listen to the victim sound in the voice of any potential partner or colleague. In fact, you can train yourself to become very astute in what the sound of someone's voice tells you about how he truly perceives himself and the world. Meditate on this for a moment and then do an experiment of actually recording or noting to yourself the undertones of the voices around you. Listen carefully to the cadence of the people you consider powerful, and then notice the voices of those you don't trust or those who are always struggling. You will see that you have an innate intuitive talent for this that you learned as a child who knew how to measure safety by sound.

The business world is truly analogous to life itself. To be well or successful, there must be no blockage in the flow of energy. Motion, velocity, frequency, and pause are the designers of quality. There must be an intuitive recognition of the "right" moment to act and the right moment to be still. The choice cannot come only, if ever, from a linear assessment, but rather from a deep connection or bonding between your consciousness and the goal. You need to activate your seventy senses to scope out the context of the project because no action is one-sided or flat. There are always infinite ramifications, matrixes, and fluctuations associated with the people involved that cue the successful person to enter into this pregnant womb and perceive the forming entity.

This always requires pause, contemplation, and receptivity— the hallmarks of the feminine. The successful person must have enough command of his or her life to take time out to listen to the inner voice of the Higher Self, which is eternally present awaiting the question. Without that meditative awareness, the vital hologram is eclipsed and you simply cannot see the truth. Taking the time to survey the hologram in this way does not need permission from anyone outside you. Wherever you are, you can create the space for such explorations, in the middle of the conference room or on a crowded freeway. Consciousness is yours; you may wield it any way you choose.

You might ask, "Show me the path that will direct me into appropriate circumstances." The answer often comes in an extraordinary and magical synchronicity that opens the way for you. Perhaps you read about something, or you get a brilliant idea, or someone gives you a great suggestion. This brings you to that fascinating clarity of "hindsight" in which you suddenly recognize the hidden elements that have been moving behind the curtain of visibility. You realize that experiences or thoughts have not been random but have been a part of a greater picture. Such clarity requires the discipline of the spiritual law of detachment.

Detachment is not inertia. On the contrary, it is the capacity to see holographically and act from the source of knowing or wait while the particulates shift into place. Sometimes it is difficult to decipher whether one is manipulating or allowing. So it is important to set your intention and let the Higher Self arrange the synergy that will bring your goal into manifestation. You then simply remain alert for the subtle indicators that mark the path and commit all your faculties to bringing it forth; only then can it happen, not before. It is a terrible misunderstanding of karma to think that you can force or deceive or maneuver reality to get what you want. The pleasure is fleeting, the residue ultimately unbearable. Though many in the business world take pleasure in the game of coercion and control, too much yang energy will lead to loneliness and painful emptiness. You must compartmentalize in order to control, and when you shut off parts of yourself, life becomes limited and eventually stale.

The yin energy knows that it can wait rather than destroy what is in the way. The holographic perspective sees all the potential energies that can be drawn into play. The future is always being fed by this moment. Even though you may be temporarily up against a brick wall, it is imperative that you work with your Higher Self and hold the "sense of success" so that it comes into manifestation, even if it appears in a form you could not have imagined. All the ups and downs of today are but the dying and the birthing of the karmic process. You can teach yourself to focus your energy beyond this trap.

Perhaps you have come up against a problem at work and you say, "I can't get around this. I can't make that person do what I want, or I can't make that project come forward." Practice the exercise of moving your consciousness beyond it, as if you have resolved it. You may find that you have already resolved it, simply by letting go or turning away from it.

For example, in the Light Institute work, we never force the Emotional Body when it thinks it is blocked. We take the focus off the point of resistance and explore something else. If the Emotional Body says, "I can't do it," we distract it just as one does a two-year-old. We say, "Let's go over here and look at this." The minute the Emotional Body turns around and starts focusing over there, the wall drops. For example, perhaps it anticipated being the victimizer, and it could not face that, so it blocked. We explore the other side of the hologram, and it says,

"Ah, thank God, I am the victim. Whew. It was not my fault, anyway."

You can be the victim if you like, because as soon as you start unwinding the energy of the victim, you are going to come right back around to the victimizer; they are inextricably bound to each other. They are dancing together. The feminine approach allows orchestration. The feminine knows that you do not have to win each battle, because you will win the war—but it may not be the most expedient choice to win the war right now. Expedience is crucial to success in business because any energy expended affects the input. Yet expedience can be very much a talent of the intuitive, to sense when something is going to be useful.

In a business arena, for example, you usually want to create something new. Let your Higher Self do the entrepreneuring by attuning your consciousness to the "feel" of that delicious awareness that comes when you pull together the vision. This brilliance of vision is never a function of the methodical linear but is a result of holographic orchestration. Our present habits of planning are simply too slow for the energies that are moving in the world today.

We must be able to focus energies that can directly influence what we are shown by the Higher Self. "How do I do it, Higher Self?" Then those sparks start to come in, and the Higher Self will say, for example, "Focus on this person." You do not realize it, but that person is a key person. Or, "The world market is going to go this way." But you cannot know that from a linear perspective; you can only perceive it when you open the hologram and allow the intuitive sense to say, "Yes, that direction." You do not know why, but your Higher Self does, because it knows that the energy currents are already influencing "probable reality" in that direction.

When you start with the little piece, suddenly everything becomes available to you, because you take the first little step and you feel fulfilled. The more you feel fulfilled, the more you risk. The more you risk, the more you contribute. And the more you contribute, the more the purpose of the soul is brought into your daily life.

It is important to commit yourself to becoming visible in your work endeavors. Observe how the CEOs and executives of companies carry themselves. You can actually palpate the air of responsibility around them. In truth, it has nothing to do with their capacities; it has to do with their own acceptance of responsibility. Far too often we get caught up in the burden of responsibility rather than the thrill inherent in taking charge or the risk of entrepreneuring. Holding the reins and taking responsibility can be wonderful if you can keep your consciousness focused on challenge.

Leaders have a way of carrying themselves that cues others to their willingness to be visible. Getting the job or contract you want has as much to do with the energetic commitment you make as it does with the actual resources you bring to the table.

From that place of leadership, you can stimulate the consciousness of other people to awaken. Then they may be more able to risk in order to do the best thing, but it falls upon you to carry the energy. Leaders are really teachers who offer models of action and presentation that allow others to discover themselves. The focus of the leader is one of becoming an open channel that can glean the truth. That is where a facility for orchestration comes in. Once you can see what is going on with the co-workers, you do not take them where they *cannot* go, you take them where they *can* go, which is often much farther than they think. The resulting productivity is inextricably entwined with the value each one places on his or her contribution to the whole. This goal of contribution is the whole core of the Nizhoni School for Global Consciousness. If you teach people to value themselves, you can enjoy watching them progress. They will make decisions that are filled with more risk, excitement, adventure, and enrichment.

Businesses are beginning to value courses related to self-exploration as they see how incredibly self-exploration can alter and transmute the entire work environment. They are beginning to understand that it is important for people to get clear about who they are and about their personal and collective goals so that they begin to realize that they can go farther by helping each other. Too many people work at boring, meaningless jobs in which they become numb and function at half speed or on automatic pilot. If you can help them find a purpose in their work, they will be much more productive. That purpose will always be about belonging and helping to make something happen. In fact, in the not-too-distant future, companies will install programs that break up the hypnotic boredom of repetitive work. Not only will there be exercise breaks and health-oriented activities, but there will be structured opportunities for contemplation to inspire inventiveness and problem-solving.

People can be taught to identify with higher consciousness. All successful businesspeople identify with the currents of energy that cue them about the best choices. Through the awareness of the seventy senses, everyone can do it.

CUES OF SYNCHRONICITY

Ninety percent of the time, great and wondrous probable realities are floating by us and we simply are too numb and too blind to see them. We do not take advantage of the infinite possibilities around us, and thus we doom ourselves to live mediocre, boring lives. We have forgotten the delightful play of nuances that gave us the cues we followed in childhood. The art of feminine synchronicity is there to point the path and to console us with the knowledge that we are guided by a supreme intelligence. We exist in an ocean of energy whose tides carry the source of life. If we become aware of the order of motion, we can ride the waves destined to strike the shore at any given moment.

What we call coincidence is the play of the Higher Self

offering guidance in its own unobtrusive way. It provides us with cues or indicators that are like warning flags or omens showing us the direction of energy. Synchronicity is the clap of thunder that startles the mind to attention. If you tune in to it, you will know immediately what is relative to you. The Higher Self speaks in shorthand, not lengthy discourses on what you should do. It will not lead you, it will present you with cues that can be deciphered to discover the truth.

Not only the Higher Self but people too cue us all the time. They let us know how they feel toward us and our projects. How often do we say "I knew that was coming"? We knew it because the Inner Female is sensitive to the myriad gestures such as voice tone, body language, spatial distances, and energies that come up around any particular person or event.

If you are contemplating a business venture, it would be of great help if you could become conscious of the energies you perceive when you consider the venture. Do you have a sense of exhilaration, brightness, a warm glow of satisfaction? Perhaps you may even notice a change in the air or see a bird soaring as you mentally survey your plan. The sights, sounds, and feelings that crop up simultaneously and share the space with your idea are all related by virtue of the great cosmic matrix wherein mind creates matter.

In order to get the brilliant idea or see the hologram so that you can go onto a level of enlightened manifestation, you have to do what was done thousands of years ago. You must seek the feminine frequencies in order to perceive the essences that open your knowing.

Try the experiment of holding an idea in your mind and simultaneously noticing what you sense around it. When you think a thought and the wind comes up at that second, it is the cue of the Higher Self saying, "Yes, that's it. Go that way!" It is the time-honored language of energy that has been used for aeons to aid the "seers." It still works today, without having to be completely shut off from the world to learn it. Because our ancestors learned it, we are given this gift through our genetic human pool.

All you have to do is be still long enough so that you can perceive what kinds of cues are there. The cues are available wherever you are. It is true in a business deal; it is true in the body. What you have to do is quicken your sensitivities, your yin relationship with all that is around you.

RELATIONSHIP

Relationship is the area most in need of transformation and transcendence in our lives. The difficulties of merging our various daily realities with those of another person cause untold stress to the vows of commitment and potential for clarity.

The coming and going of daily life creates tremendous disruption to any kind of profound communication. The constant separation and reuniting leaves us dealing with mostly exterior levels of relating and takes up a major portion of relationship. This brings with it attendant anxiety about future connection. With the Emotional Body preoccupied by this insecurity, it is difficult to train the mind to dwell on the positive. Marriages fail today very much because we have not learned how to sustain relationships without constant physical touch. It is tremendously difficult for the two of you to merge into one being when your whole identity is based on how well you succeed in whatever your individual activity dictates for the major portion of your waking hours and you are then expected to shift that identity to match someone who suddenly reappears in your life at the end of the day.

The incessant inner chatter about being chosen or avoiding pain steers us ever more into the shadow side of the self. In fact, nowhere else in our lives do we relinquish more of the self because of our hunger to be loved or acknowledged.

You can train your consciousness to relieve the fears of the

Emotional Body by actually developing the ability to contact the ones you love psychically. Perhaps you sit in an office all day long, but you want to keep the wonderful feelings you shared with your mate. At any moment you can simply open the pineal channel of psychic communication and perceive what your partner is doing or feeling. Send a little message via the beams of color and feel how it is received. It creates an excitement, a playfulness, that enhances your sense of connection. Later, when you meet your loved one, you have already created a charge of energy that helps you switch gears easily and dissolve the residue of office chatter so that you are completely present.

The problem of carrying the office home is a present danger in many relationships. It creates an aftershock effect in which you are still occupied with work-related issues and feel unable to give importance to what is happening at home. This causes family members to feel devalued and out of touch with you, resulting in battles under the guise of something different from the simple human need to be important to someone.

All these antics sap the energy systems. If at work you are daydreaming about relationship, and at night you are rehashing the events of the day, there is no space for the present. There is a great difference between daydreaming and transmission of energy. Daydreaming is an avoidance technique that allows one to muse about a desired reality. Conscious energy transmission is an action of clear intent that brings the mind to an alert state. Within this peaceful holographic awareness, the feminine frequencies transmit all knowing. It is a conscious intention that allows the mind to embrace it but does not stem from the limitation of the mind.

When you first begin to tune in to your loved ones from a distance, you may suffer a bit of static in the channel, causing you to feel vague anxiety signals. Often you worry because something is triggered by association, something in your Emotional Body that you project onto them. These are really leftover fears about something bad happening to you. If you get a worry message, send your loved ones the color energy that will give them the kind of support they need to help them through the experiences they have chosen. That is all you can do. Worrying is simply a contract or bondage that says "I have to worry about you because if you are not okay, I am not okay." This karmic mirroring is not the true source of relationship.

Men and women are always worrying, "Does she still love me?" or, "Is he looking at someone else?" If you are sending loving energies back and forth, that kind of dialogue will disappear from the arena of relationship. The moment you become the abundant giver, there is no need to worry. You cannot have what is not yours. Also, you can only keep what you give away. When you love someone, you must honor that person's freedom to choose the needed experiences. At every moment you must set your loved one free. If you do and you still have karma together, that person will always come toward you.

If you indeed sensed something negative coming from people you love, it could only present itself through the laws of attraction by which on some level they have called it. It could not have been an accident. They must have made a choice to experience it, and it is a choice only they can make. Your role is to send the supporting energy they need to make that choice! Each person must be free enough to risk, which entails a sense of power and abundance. If you are abundant, you can give it away. Because you give it away, you are free and can take a new step.

Unfortunately, giving is often entwined with hidden agendas and mixed messages: "I will send this to you, but you must give me something back." As long as you are holding on, trying to get someone to give back to you, you will be blocked by the terrible illusion of emotional debt. You become vulnerable to anxiety: "If I don't have you, I won't survive." The most difficult lesson is learning that no one ultimately can fulfill you except your own Higher Self.

Women are especially subject to the projection onto others for creating fulfillment in life. It is a double-edged sword, because they consequently feel that their own reality is not worthy enough. The mundane tasks of homemaking pale even in comparison with the boring tasks of the office because there is no one to play them off. Women want company, and thus the superficial conversations at work seem more satisfying than isolation.

If you can hold your attention on yourself, whatever you are doing is important enough. It is only you who need acknowledge your endeavors. All boredom has to do with disconnection from the self. You are bored because nobody is doing it for you and you do not dare go out and do something that you feel is more than you can handle. This is excessive yin passivity coupled with negative yang judgment. Boredom comes from fear. It comes from suspended animation, inertia—the inertia to risk being alive because you are judging yourself too much: "If I do that, I might not be accepted by the outside world, so I had better not do it. Therefore, I can do nothing." This is why we have mediocrity rather than brilliance. It is everywhere in the world—in business, education, the environment: mediocrity, the great human disease!

The fusion of yin and yang opens a whole new potential of manifestation. It is the blending of knowing and doing. Are you ready to say "I will do it"? Not "My Higher Self will do it" or "My partner [or my boss] will do it"—"I will do it"? The moment you give permission to do or be it, incredible insights come to you: "Ah! Here is a way to do it!" As yin and yang merge, the question and answer find each other.

As you take that initial step, volition begins and the next ripple shows itself. These are the energetic spirals that carry the rivers of evolution out to the great cosmic sea. You take the step and then the Higher Self will show you how it creates the next. Suddenly you realize the choices involved in going this way or that. It is the willingness to engage that transforms you.

The imprint in this universe has been focused on the masculine, which expresses the doing. We have succumbed to the illusion that we are only that which we manifest. The truth is that we only do because of our being. The doing is just the way that we play with our being.

In the Western world, we have become stuck in the judgment of the doing. Instead of just using the doing as part of the play, we seem to have lost its playmate, the knowing. It is like falling onto one side of the equation. If we can just remember that childlike quality saying "I will try it." Wisdom emerges from experience. The knowing energy comes out to engage life and thus initiates the progression. It has to take form to create the spark that brings cause and effect, which is the pulsation of life.

Do not worry if you make a mistake, because out of your "mistake" will come the next ripple. The only way you can become successful or arrive at your goal is through motion. You have to take a step. It makes no difference what direction you take. You may feel that you picked the wrong person for a relationship, but there are no mistakes. By entering into proximity with someone, your emotional karma will move you. You discover what you want or do not want; or you become aware if you are repeating a pattern. You cannot be damaged by this learning process, you can only be enlightened.

As you become more aware, the quality of what you manifest will change. Thus the outer reality is created to fit the inner truth. Though they are interdependent, the yin, inward direction sets the charge for outer motion. It is the yin that becomes laden with the weight of static existence and seeks growth through yang expression.

Seeking outside is a yang concept. "This does not fulfill me" is the echo heard in homes around the country. It does not fulfill you because you are crying out for the world to acknowledge you. It is so painful to fall into the trap of evaluating and judging through the yang manifestation of "How many things I have been successful at today?" What is really important is the grace with which you were successful. If you express with integrity, every endeavor is successful because of the quality of your intention. On the other hand, if the accomplishments were gained by manipulation of others, the glory will soon be clouded by their avoidance of you.

It is difficult to face our manipulation. That is why it angers us when somebody else says, "You are manipulating." We hate it when anybody sees what we are hiding from ourselves. Sometimes you may be tempted to pretend you are getting something from the Higher Self, when in fact it is coming from the Emotional Body.

If you get a little jerk in your solar plexus because you want it to happen in the way you are invested, your body will cue you to its emotional source. Your attachment to it is the sign of the Emotional Body. Attachment is a very physical sensation. It feels like bonding energy that forces a spatial relationship that you may cling to resist. The desperate hope that you could somehow control things with your will is utter illusion.

The cosmic joke is that you can only control what your karma has designed to create in the first place. Each circumstance you create with your will is a teacher to you. Learning is not dangerous because you are untouchable. You are constantly changing, therefore you need not force another to your will. Control is always about fear; it strangles spontaneity until, immobile, you atrophy and die.

If the Emotional Body is saying "I need a partnership, but I must have control," it will be so limited that it cannot truly risk having one, yet it will suffer tremendously in its prison of loneliness. Fortunately, there is a difference between choice and need. You can choose something without needing it to be a certain way. You can choose a partnership for what it will teach you, thereby taking responsibility and relinquishing the outcome because it will be okay no matter how it comes out. Choosing implies responsibility that can never take you into the space of the victim.

What will ease this longing is spiritual energy, the sense of the soul finding purpose and meaning in every experience that floods through it, dissolving the illusion of separation and need.

If you open your consciousness to the hologram, the limitless energy will nourish you enough so that you forget the clutches of need.

Whenever you are hungry for love, simply stop a minute and ask your body what it feels like to be loved. The body retains hundreds of different imprints of the sensation of love. When you start generating what it feels like to be loved, you do not have to have a partner. When you do not have to have a partner, that is when you get one.

7

MULTI-INCARNATIONAL MAN

There are many theories about consciousness and fields of influence that include morphic resonance, reincarnation, and collective unconscious, all of which describe a pooling or recognition of experiences that are more than the individual body's frame of reference. All share the extension of the time factor that allows experience to disengage itself from an illusionary treadmill of time and roam free to seek that which enhances the soul.

The multi-incarnational format in which we see the different bodies we have had of both genders is tremendously helpful to bring these experiences into consciousness so that we can recognize why we are the way we are now. Using this format, we can release experiences or conclusions of the Emotional Body that are destructive to us. There are so many associations that do not seem to be coming from our own body or that could not be considered to be ours from the present-day perspective, but which are nevertheless a part of inexplicable experiences whereby we know things and feel déjà-vu. These remembrances often create confusion when they leak through into our present experience and we are consciously unable to remember them or to fix them in context.

We are conceived by the mixing of genetic material from both mother and father. On the level of the chromosomes, these energies from the female and the male merge and provide reference to the attributes of both physiologies. Each parent contributes the essence that the developing fetus will have as resource material for the male and female energies it will use in life. We do not consciously realize these inheritances, yet they are there influencing our lives, however subtly. Our sense of a personal relationship with each body seems to go beyond a simple inheritance. The body and all its trillions of cells have recordings of experiences that relate to the polarity body, or opposite gender, in intimate ways that are not merely passed down from the parent but are our very own.

At the Light Institute, we are never concerned with someone's belief system about multi-incarnations but are interested in what their body can express to them. Many people grow up amid deep unresolved conflicts with their body because it behaves in ways they consider to be appropriate only to the opposite sex. The recognition that we have had many bodies, both male and female, explains a lot of the confusion that men and women have about physical or sexual expression in their bodies.

In today's world both men and women are overly concerned with the presentation of their bodies. Ultimately it is a disaster to define the self by the measure and merit of the body because it will one day fade away and leave you with the uncertainties of middle age. The emotional etiology of the "masculine menopause"—in which one is gripped by the fear of losing all physical prowess and thus embarks upon the game of decoy and cover— is well documented around the world. The forty-year-old man begins to seek something to replace what he feels he has lost by enhancing his sense of self with externals: new job, new wife, new body. Although exercise is a key to body renewal, the driving overexertion many men fall into is due to anxiety about their masculinity rather than a communion with the body and its actual needs.

PROJECTION ONTO WOMEN

One day soon, perhaps, we will all learn to honor the body's great gift of life and accept its male/female duet with more grace. There is profound anxiety about the presence of feminine energy in many, many men. They have a sense of the feminine within them that longs to be expressed. Unfortunately this feminine urge causes men to project heavily onto women because the woman inside the man is so hungry to be alive. In the midst of stifling his Inner Female the man tries desperately to get the females around him to act out his feminine energy the way he feels it should be expressed in accordance with how it lives covertly in him. The man unconsciously identifies with all the women in his life, seeking his own feminine experience through them. Since his repertoire comes from his maternal inheritance as well as his own multi-incarnational memories, his attempt to project onto the outside woman is unsuccessful, and he is left with a deep anxiety he cannot recognize. It could never be a perfect fit. In an attempt to find the woman within himself, he becomes intertwined emotionally with the woman outside him. He thinks it is somehow about her, when it is only about what is inside himself. At the same time he is projecting onto her, he is weathering her projection onto him of her Inner Male.

However, men today are beginning to be reactionary about the loud, incessant noises made by the women in their life over women's lib issues: equality at work and at home and demands for communication and emotional support. After allowing generations of pressure on men to maintain an image of the strong, invincible protector who would take care of everything, women are now commandeering a change to the sensitive male who will let them express at least some of the power. Unfortunately, women are still unsure what that kind of male looks and feels like, and they still want assurance that the man is not too weak for them. Mixed messages are the result, coupled with confusion and anxiety about what it is to be a male.

The answer lies in recognition of the multidimensional self

that can consciously use any aspect of an extensive repertoire to respond to relationship from a place of true center. Trust yourself, you are all you need to be, and the person you pick to play the role opposite you is teaching you how to hone the traits that most suit you.

It is too easy to project on the woman, thinking she is demanding something you are not sure you have and therefore feeling angry and anxious, especially if you are unconsciously looking for the female within. The truth is that women want the same things men do from relationship: love, nurturing, support, and acknowledgment.

I have often been fascinated by how many relationships succeed in which the female plays the masculine part and the male explores his creative nature in depth. What is important is to pursue your own true self rather than become imbedded in the mask or the facade of what a male "should" be like.

The down side of the human trait to be in company, in group, is always to be engrossed in finding out or satisfying what others think you should be like. Far too many men and women waste their energy hoping to be chosen by someone else. Nothing is more tragic than men posturing for females who really don't know what they need men to be like because they are desperately trying to discover what it is to be a woman.

The best solution would be to skip this side road and go directly to the place where each could look upon the other as a soul friend with whom the dance could be wild or slow or any way we choose, according to our soul's purpose.

Little boy children will often emulate the characteristics of feminine expression in their mothers, aunts, grandmothers, and teachers, hoping to find an avenue for the energy that feels so comfortable, so natural, within themselves.

When men come to the Light Institute to clear their families, the grandmothers or the aunts often take up a tremendous space of unresolved experiences and relationships, simply because of the psychic mirroring and the profound influence that the feminine energy has upon a small male child. A little boy feels the receptive connection and telepathic communion shared by females that are so often denied by the males around him. His access to his father, his uncles, to the men in the family, is expressed mostly by activity. He is encouraged to communicate through sports or projects that are externalized rather than expressions of his inner world. To the small child, the inner dimensions are still integral to his reality even though he is unable to articulate his perceptions to the world around him.

It is interesting to note how often little boys playing dress-up choose to wear the clothes of the mother or the sister rather than the father. Some of this may be because there is a flamboyance allowed women that children spontaneously enjoy.

Women are conscious and sensitive to the colors they choose and the styles and fabrics they wear as expressions of their mood and their feelings. Because small children are sensitive to emotion, mood, and feeling, they identify with these feminine qualities and love to drape themselves in these energies.

A small child is so fluid, elastic, ready to try on many different guises of the self to see what it is like to be this way, to be that way; to be the warrior, to be the mother. Even the boy child feels more comfortable with the fluid nature of the woman, who is more changing and versatile. He senses profoundly her power as well, because she is so much the giver of life, and all children understand that innate power.

The male child, therefore, has normally only the mother to model these things, which are so easily learned by him because she expresses recognition of his subtle emotions and feelings. The world for the child is built upon these recognitions and capacities, and if the father does not enter into them or does not express such subtleties, even in his auric field, the child then tends to become more attached and attuned to the mother, if she will allow it. Sometimes the mother denies her boy child the space to express psychic and sensitive awareness because of her fear that the father will reject him for not being "manly." She may be equally invested in the child behaving in masculine ways and even project onto her small son her need to relate to the yang energy outside herself.

FATHERING

The connection with the mother may be a source of pain and confusion for the father from the perspective of the ego, because it reinforces the reality of his distance from other people in his life. Children are very physical and need to be embraced and caressed and stroked. It is important for fathers to allow themselves to embrace their children. In so doing, their own, perhaps hidden, emotions, tenderness, and sensitivities are awakened and begin to surface. Fathering can be such a great learning opportunity for transformation in the lives of men. When they enter into the world that was formerly only the domain of mothers and women, they are able to access their own feminine energy.

It is beautiful to see a father nurturing and expressing his love through psychic attunement to his child. During the entire gestation period, the fetus has already had access to the psychic-emotional fields of the father through the cells that spun off from the sperm. The newborn knows his father as well as he knows his mother, though the association to the father has less physical survival energy attached to it. We so often describe the role of the father as that of the protector, when in fact it is the other way around: the mother is the one who orchestrates physical well-being, and the father holds access to unseen worlds! Because so few men are aware of this, the psychic channels between them and their children shut down rather quickly once the child has been born. The unending variety of stimuli from the third dimension draws the child into our material world, and since the fathers so rarely respond to psychic messages, the little one holds these gateways open through the mother, if at all.

Imprints at Birth

If a man is able to be at the birth and become a part of the birthing process, a bonding takes place that allows for the activation of his maternal instincts, his repertoire of mothering. Rather than having to fight these inner feelings because of insecurity about their being acceptable or allowable to his concept of himself as a male, he experiences the divine rush of oneness that heals the pain of being only the witness.

When the child experiences the birth of a new sibling, he feels the mystery, the anxiety, the reverence, of the parents and relatives. He perceives that this is, indeed, an important event and takes in all of the energies that are related to the birth. The child experiences his mother emerging from this initiation after which there is a profound, if short-lasting, change in her sense of herself, accompanied by a psychic opening of her etheric body that takes place when she gives birth. This opening lasts for about six weeks after the birth. It matters not whether the delivery was an easy or a difficult one; we all have an emotional and psychic recognition of this mystery of life that is so intimately connected with the woman. We must acknowledge that in the nature of birthing lies a great magic, a magnificent power that cannot be stolen or usurped from the woman. The power to birth is at the core of life itself, and though we may not use it so voluminously in the future, it must always carry with it a great energy that will continue to inspire us all.

Remerging with the Inner Mother/Inner Female

Little boys are fascinated by birth, and men hold the longing to be a part of it deep within their being. When, at last, through multi-incarnational work, a man is able to reunite with this mystical, magical part of himself, great healing takes place.

During sessions with the Inner Mother, men have the opportunity to experience birth directly. Through the awakening of the mother within, the man can attune on the cellular level to the myriad sensations of pregnancy and birth, feeling the emotional, physical, and spiritual changes that take place during the creative process. It is a rich and satisfying sensation for a man to feel himself suckling a baby. These sessions are accompanied with deep emotion and often the release of tears. Afterward he always has an unforgettable look in his eye that communicates a new awareness of life. Feeling complete within himself, he rushes off to share his exuberance with his family and fellow colleagues.

I remember one male client who was the oldest of six children. Because of family difficulties, he found himself in the mothering role and practically raised his five siblings himself, daily feeding and bathing the little ones. His greatest pain was that no matter what he did, he felt he couldn't give them the nurturing he wanted to give. Although he did an admirable job from the perspective of others, he always felt inadequate and frustrated. When he finally found himself suckling a baby in a beautiful lifetime as a female, he wept profusely as at last he was able to encounter what it was he had wanted to do that was related to his desire to nurture.

The sessions with the Inner Female and the Inner Male have such a profound transformative effect that even I am sometimes startled. For a man, it is one of the most revolutionary experiences to feel, from the inside, what a woman feels. A man who experiences lovemaking from the body of a female will go on to a totally new octave of embracing and merging as he now has within his frame of reference the feelings and sensations of it from the female perspective. What an incredible opening takes place as he feels what it is like to be penetrated, to feel surrender on the level of the body and the heart! There is no sexual manual or even book of tantra that can compare with the experience of intimate knowing in the body.

When a man explores himself as a woman, he understands, perhaps for the first time, the potential of relationship. He knows what his mate is seeking from him and how to give it to her.

What he often finds shocking is how different he appears from the female side of himself. This bilateral view is the prerequisite for merging the male and the female in a new dance of relationship. Each year at the Light Institute we receive many letters from wives who write in utter amazement about the transformation of their husbands after the Inner Female sessions. They speak of renewed and vastly enhanced communication on intimate and psychic levels.

These are my favorite series of sessions because they catalyze such dramatic changes in individuals, relationships, and lifestyles. The man who has awakened his nurturing essence wants to touch it again and again. He begins to reach out to the world with a tenderness that has gone beyond the battle stations of masculine etiquette. He loses the stiffness that so often characterizes a man's attempts to express caring, especially toward other men.

Feminine Energies in the Homosexual

Much of a man's hunger to access the feminine within comes from a cellular memory of the female that infiltrates his present body. The cellular recordings are not limited to those of his mother but are actually his own. Often, when a man has been a woman in his very last lifetime, that memory may overshadow the experiences he is having at this time.

It is common in homosexuals for the imprints of the body's experience as a woman simply to override the present reality. This is one of the reasons male homosexuals often seem to have the temperament of a woman. The mirroring effect comes into play here again, whereby the male homosexual carries a fascination for the female because he is unconsciously experiencing the female as a mirror of his own emotional self. He may enjoy the company of women as a mirror, a mirror that he can gesticulate in front of, through his own feminine expression. The feminine psyche has a rich repertoire and is easily recorded by the Emotional Body. But when there is a strong emotional makeup, it is very difficult to express within the limitations and cultural restrictions of male form.

The hormonal balance in the homosexual often predisposes the pineal gland to function more on the psychic levels. This tends to anchor the Emotional Body deeper into the initial psychic relationship shared with the father. Though there is always psychic communication with the mother, it goes on in an integrated way combined with neurological and physiological shared activity. With the father, the biological contact is mostly the echo of the genetic inheritance. Thus, the baby stretches out its psychic and spiritual antennae to contact a part of the self that is not immediately available within the womb but that nevertheless whispers its energetic reality to the child.

The gay person often suffers throughout his life because he feels this unspoken connection, which is not addressed by his father, who may never have been aware of it on conscious levels. He tends to become stuck in a relentless struggle to win the father's approval or attention because deep within his core he remembers that channel of communication from before his birth. The father truly does not comprehend what the son is seeking. His father's seeming denial of him strikes at the source of his trust and sense of himself so that, emotionally, he cannot go on to establish other kinds of relationships because this primary relationship has not been confirmed on the level he knows it to be.

Energetically, homosexuals are functioning with male and female attributes that require a merging of their characteristics in order to create a harmonic and whole self. As the male and female come together within the same body, a profound spiritual consciousness often emerges. One day all males must dare to express this spiritual energy. When they do, there will be a new respect given to those who can demonstrate the value of these two energies in concert with each other.

Imprints of the Inner Female

It is exquisite when a man can surrender to the feminine energy within him and be able to express it in his daily life. The experiences of the Inner Female definitely formulate the patterns of expression of the feminine within a man in terms of quality and style. She offers him a rich tapestry of subjective material to formulate his inner perspective. However, whatever her emotional imprints at the hands of life, they will find their way into his covert habits of present response. This is how the negative feminine finds such a powerful ally in a man with strong feminine traits. For example, if he has had lifetimes in which seduction was the only available path for expression of the feminine powers, he will manifest this negative feminine energy as a part of his way of being now. If he had experiences as a female in which he was abused or unloved, he will tend to equate his feminine energy with the denial of love. It is a vicious circle in which he senses that the female in him will not be loved and so concludes this to be so, even when there is evidence to the contrary. This tends to create a love/hate relationship between himself and his Inner Female. Thus, when the female emerges, he meets her with overreactive or destructive masculine force, attempting to overpower her so that he will not be hurt. His mechanism of denial is often a seemingly impenetrable mask that conveys a hardness and an aggressive exterior that belies his inner core.

To bring the consciousness to a point of merging where fusion is possible, you must truly be able to experience inside yourself that which you have hitherto sought outside you. Contacting the Inner Female, as we learned to do in chapter 5, is a most powerful way to dissolve the projection onto the outside female and therefore end the confusion of those amorphic experiences and emotions you have within.

When you allow the Inner Female to take form, you can access that energy in its pure state and allow it to give expression in your daily life. It is a most fascinating exploration of your unconscious, to use the power of symbology and inner vision to

come directly into communion with that Inner Female and discover where the reference points of feminine energy are either
entangled within you or are freely flowing.

For example, if the Inner Female comes up looking like a
"slut," for the first time you will be able to access the subconscious
levels that you relate to your sexual energy. Her image immediately taps you into the thought forms and emotions you hold
about the feminine and your relationship to it. You can perceive
if she is characterized by any stereotypical judgments such as
"Women are sluts, dangerous sexually [should be a nun, should
be on a pedestal, should be a saint, only our mothers . . .]," or
any of those points of reference of the feminine. Each time you
ask the Inner Female to take form, you come face to face with
either your own feminine harmony or your separation to that
most Divine Source. If there is an emotional charge or stereotypical presentation of her, you can immediately rebalance the
energy through the technique of gift exchange while simultaneously looking directly into the heart of your experiential truth.
As you work with her, she is able to imbue you with the quality
of energy that is absolutely appropriate at any moment to enhance
your expression of compassion, creativity, and merging.

8

OUT OF THE RIB

The biblical story of the emergence of woman from the rib of man echoes a universally held belief that women are weaker and second to men, not only in strength, but in their capacity to meet the world. The overriding impression has always been that women should be sheltered underneath the protective wing of men.

In a world controlled by conquer and thrust, the major role of the feminine energy has been to support and guide from behind the scenes. At last there is a stirring of an evolutionary shift that is propelling the yin feminine energy from its inaccessible source toward the periphery of manifestation, into the terrain of the male. This emergence is occurring with a foreseeable wobble, causing the newly visible female to pretend the attributes of the masculine model, which in reality are foreign to our own essence.

As these energies come forward, the woman has taken on the mask of the male in order to appear strong and powerful enough to stand alone. This is a terrible misunderstanding and does a disservice to our own sacred energies. The yang model has led the world to the brink of disaster, and it is the yin that must now come forward and reverse the damage by awakening the consciousness of humanity. Although that yin energy can be expressed by male leaders, there is a rising tide of women who are beginning to take up positions of power and dissolve old inept formats for governing life.

This chapter is for you women. You may smile as you discover some of your old games and resolve to come out from the rib with humor, honesty, and a deep commitment to use the spiritual source, so much a natural part of your heritage, to gift the world!

RELATIONSHIP

It is not the nature of the female to stand alone or foster separation. Her entire body is set in the pattern to create more of the self, to form relationship. Ours is the innate vibration of inclusion, which is exactly what is urgently needed in today's world: the awareness of individual relationship to the whole.

What keeps women in life and in body is relationship. One of the reasons there have not been more women spiritual leaders in the past is that there is a strong energy in a woman's body to produce a family, to have a partner, a mate. For aeons women have carried imprints that have whispered, "You must belong to the tribe or you will not survive." Those imprints are no longer valid today, and women have begun to seek definition in a new way.

Yet any variation on the family theme usually places women in a situation of aloneness. This newfound independence can be terribly frightening because we have not learned to validate ourselves by our internal recognition but, rather, only from external validation—whether we are attractive physically or are able to answer the needs of others.

Women seek verification every bit as much as men do; it is simply more difficult for us because the standard is not the same. In pain and frustration women so often plead, "Please see me— not my form, not my mind, but my soul!" even though we ourselves don't know what we mean and are attempting to describe something we only feel deeply within.

Relationship is the cornerstone of feminine energy. Therefore we are much more willing to surrender the struggle for power to another, simply because our hunger to communicate is stronger than our need for control. As a result, we all too often surrender to limitation rather than striking out to create something new. In our great urge to connect with someone outside ourselves, we engage in almost any kind of conversation or encounter just for the momentary touch that communication gives us. We deploy all manner of decoys in order to gain a moment's company. Consider the tradition of "taking tea," borrowing from the neighbor, making love for the embrace afterward, asking for help on a project not because we truly need it, but for the pleasure of togetherness. We are extremely expedient in terms of establishing a base for relationship.

It would behoove us instead to see when one energy is not in concert with another, to let go of energies that do not create a whole. We stay too long in old patterns of relationship, especially with our own children, rather than following the evolutionary process of maturation and growth and letting go of each being as that time comes. We have a tendency to "make do" rather than realize that we could instigate new avenues of relationship by insisting on mutual exploration. In part, it is a "comfortable misery" of habitual daily patterns and contacts with husbands and families that does not wish to say good-bye to the advantages of monetary and emotional rewards. The trouble is we don't recognize the bind of limitation these amenities bring that holds closed the gateway to the new.

Women deal with these limitations by projecting onto relationships. We have an affinity for making others who are important to us bigger than life, seeing qualities in them that we want to see in order to rationalize our investment in the relationship. We convince ourselves that we must have that relationship in order to be fulfilled, when we could have picked anybody else to play that role. In reality there are thousands of souls who carry the vibration facilitating any particular karmic relationship to occur.

Women, much more than men, are voyeurs. We can get a

great deal of pleasure out of fantasizing about what could be real. A potentially boring and unexciting relationship can be revamped by matching it to one we see someone else going through. Like women matching menstruation cycles, we will use our Emotional Body to create a drama similar to the one a friend is experiencing, just for the sake of the adventure! If we would sincerely explore these truths, we could more easily let go and surmount projection. Because it is the Emotional Body that designs these qualities of interchange, it is very important to search out the spiritual roots, not the emotional cravings of relationship.

I remember a close friend of mine who became infatuated with a handsome Native American man who lived outside of Santa Fe. She was married and so did not want to engage in an affair, but she became totally absorbed in her fantasy of what it would be like to live with him by reading everything Indian as well as becoming involved in native arts and crafts. Ultimately even being inundated with all the things that represented his reality could not fill the hole she felt in her life. She was struck with a rare, nondescript rheumatoid condition that put her in bed for several weeks. I felt it was her longing that was causing her lapse of happy will and spoke to her of the pitfalls of projection. We began to explore the things she identified in him for which she hungered so ardently.

We opened up her multi-incarnational memories and found that she had experienced a lifetime as an Indian man in which she had a powerful connection with the earth and the Great Spirit. Discovering that this magical being was *within her* helped dissolve her projection onto her friend. It was so interesting to realize that what she had interpreted in sexual terms was really her own romance with Mother Nature and the powerful male within her self! Shortly afterward she was well again and out in the woods with a full heart and an intact marriage.

This projecting quality causes us all to spend a great deal of our energy maneuvering family or friends and orchestrating the play of life, when sometimes it would be wiser, rather than molding other, to let new relationships evolve. But it is difficult for us to let go. Long after it is all over and we are with someone else, we will remember and carry with us the emotions and conversations of old relationships.

Women are more vengeful than men. The negative feminine is more acutely sensitive to any threats that have to do with the subtle domain of control and yet will keep a relationship going, sometimes to ensure that we have the last say. We would rather console ourselves with an occasional dig and often expend great energy thinking about what we should have said or would counter in an argument, rather than discontinuing the relationship. Part of that comes from the feminine habit of taking whatever there is and moving it around, rather than the masculine concept of simply finding something new.

The saving grace comes from recognizing that the need to maneuver others stems from the fear of being judged by them. It is a classical female maneuver to project onto the male and insist that he does not allow change, rather than acknowledge the responsibility to make necessary changes oneself.

You have an Inner Male who can help you reach the visible with your knowing, your loving, your protective qualities that enhance relationship. However, the Inner Male must be used in concert with the Inner Female so that it is not the separate or aggressive self that comes forward attempting to compete, out-maneuver, or force another in order to seek and express the self. If, however, you have discovered your Inner Male, you will be able to take the initiative and shape your relationships the way you wish them to be, without dependence on outside approval.

Why don't you take a moment to bring your Inner Male into your consciousness so that you can have a feel for his expression in your life at this moment? Do this in the same manner you did with your Inner Female in chapter 5.

ALONENESS

Perhaps one of the biggest blind spots on the horizon of enlightenment is the acknowledgment that ultimate fulfillment can never come from a source outside the self. Women are reluctant to strike out for new openings because we are afraid of the stigma of being alone. There is still an unspoken yet deep-seated imprint that it is only a loser who has not been chosen by a man, a feeling of guilt or unworthiness associated with being alone. Society has veiled its notion that an unattended female is a threat to home and family and so discourages and discriminates against women who choose to be alone.

Men, on the other hand, experience great aloneness even while being surrounded by family because they hold so much inside and keep their inner self separate. They are taught a competitive energy that includes aloneness—king of the mountain: "It is either you or me. It is not us together." From the beginning of time they have been taught all the war games that made it more acceptable, even heroic, for them to be alone. This process is still going on today—are not your young boys playing games of war?

Issues of aloneness come up for women in their late forties and fifties when their identity as the mother, and even the wife, begins to fall away. Often there is divorce at that time, and it seems that fate has dealt a cruel blow because the woman may not feel that her seductive qualities will serve as a lure for relationship.

This is the Higher Self's way of prodding, of helping us recognize that only now can all the powers of the yin come forward, uncompromised by the buying and selling of seduction or sexuality. These yin powers are of great value in their own right; the one who has always played the supporting role, either as confidante to others or partner to man, mother to children, suddenly can take on a new integrated role as teacher, as the one who can now become the keeper of the gate between spiritual worlds and everyday life.

That is a major role for women today, to teach our children as well as our partners how to access profound levels of human potential to enrich life, to avoid the pitfalls of the Emotional Body by lifting it up out of the octaves of hunger and need.

We women must now acknowledge ourselves as the true teachers of our children. If we are to create new kinds of relationships, we must relate differently to our children. We can free them from the role playing that so inhibits the expression of their soul and causes them feelings of deep isolation. To treat the boy child as if he were something special is ultimately a disservice because he grows up thinking he must prove to the world that he is special and worries that he, in fact, is not. To be expected to perform in a certain way is a great burden and usually leads to anxiety. Girls should be raised without comparison in value to boys. The archaic idea that producing a boy is more prestigious because it somehow makes the father more manly hearkens back to the Dark Ages when soldiers and frontiersmen were at a premium.

When the mother can look at the child and acknowledge both the male and female within that child, she can be instrumental in the balancing of those energies, without confusion on the part of the child, but with acceptance of all human expression.

As we women learn to tune inside to our spiritual nature, we can dissolve the hunger brought about by loneliness. The spiritual bliss of communion with the self circumvents the static of the mind or the casual sacrifice of the body in order to avoid feeling alone. When we begin to touch our own spiritual energy, that hunger for relationship is resolved and we experience completeness.

I wonder how many of you are daydreaming of a partner or feeling wasted because you are not at this moment in relationship. The moment you feel a tug of loneliness, just stop and feel your Inner Male, or let your Inner Child play with you, or ask the energy of your Higher Self to caress you. Within minutes you will feel differently and be able to continue with your life—which has more value than you could ever know, until you begin to see how you can use its power through accessing the inner worlds.

It is often difficult for us to move into the exterior world without denying our most powerful ally, the intuitive consciousness. We are afraid to be challenged about something others can't see. We quickly learn to adapt a public persona that allows us to hide. Many women control their relationships by misusing their psychic capacities. Now is the moment for women to acknowledge these subtle energies that can bring them into prominence as a force capable of healing the planet. Women now have a new freedom from the stereotypical mandate of identification as the mother or wife or even career person. As people around the world seek a new expression of the self, the multifaceted energy of relationship can become a powerful tool for peace.

THE BODY GAME

The body performs a powerful role in the experience of womanhood. The intricate variety of hormones that are in play to facilitate reproduction directly stimulate the Emotional Body. The negative side of this is the overreactive emotional upheavals that women experience as the result of hormonal secretion and that cause them to engage in manipulation. The positive is the strong emotional capacity for relationship.

The interweaving of the physical body with all the subtle energetics that then influence the spirit and Emotional Body makes for a profound experience of the difference between separation and merging. When we are touching bodies, all that is real converges at that point of the touch. Both women and men will stay in relationships out of the need to be touched, even though everything else is off. People who can't even converse can reach each other with their touch. The intent of touch changes as we grow in life. By the time we are adults, we have a whole repertoire of touch: touches for mothering, for encouragement, camaraderie, consoling, tenderness, seduction.

Young girls begin to practice the art of seduction within their first five years. They are applauded and encouraged by their families, who think it charming that they can so easily captivate their daddies and friends. (These early imprints that associate success with approval by men set the stage for deep-rooted anxiety about self-worth when the seductive assets ultimately fade.) This unabashed flirtation takes on a new twist at puberty when the body enters the play. What was once merely a game of behavior becomes a dynamic energetic at puberty.

Awakened by a new driving energy, the body, like the wild flower, hurries to reproduce itself. Its urgent potential whispers encouragement to the subconscious of the female to find a mate. This creates the deep impression that fulfillment is bonded to attracting and holding a male partner. It is the voice of the primordial physical body, not the more shallow craving for pleasure, that is speaking. Women become stuck in the octave of seduction, whereby the entire self is encased in the idea that it must clutch tightly to the male. Our dependence on the male would not be so great but for the profound fear of aloneness that is echoing from bodily levels of species survival. I find that this whisper to snatch a mate becomes a roar at about twenty-six years of age when the biological clock for reproduction begins ticking. (It happens to men around twenty-eight or twenty-nine years of age, when the astrological Saturn return occurs. They become aware of a sense of emptiness, and they look for a wife.)

Thus, women have learned to buy and sell, to barter the self. We engage in contracts, vows, and manipulation of subtle energies, sexual energies, in order to place ourselves in an environment of worth. This is especially evident in relation to sexual activities. We have been willing to use the body in the marketplace, not because physical sensations are reportedly so wonderful, but because of the need to feel some tenderness, to find a place to connect so as not to be alone. On a physical level, this has cost us dearly. In all of the "arrangements" of the body, whenever the feelings of the heart are not blended with the sexual energy, the auric field wilts. It does not regain its strength for about forty-eight hours while the Emotional Body must attempt to process out all the extraneous emotional and energetic materials that have entered it from the partner. Even when we love someone, our auric fields inextricably entwine. If the love energy is compatible, the auric fields do not wilt but still carry the energy of the partner.

Females used to fare better sexually than men because we were on the receiving end of the physical exchange. We were able to draw in those magnificent juices and energies coming from the sperm that lent power and life force. With the advent of condoms, much of the energy is now blocked and thus not received. This can be overcome as lovers learn to extend love from all their chakras, but it must be a very conscious endeavor.

We females have been given the opportunity for multiple orgasms. Unfortunately we often do not discover this until we reach our sexual prime between thirty-six and forty years of age. Having orgasms definitely changes our focus. This is the time when we women most commonly take on lovers and become insecure, because our concern about desirability relates directly to the increasing sexual urge.

As we awaken to our sexual energy, a great anxiety comes up as suddenly we feel a hunger of sexual merging on a physical level. Rather than taking the sexuality and going deeper, we search for a way to fit these new stirrings into our life. By that time our habit of projection is strong and our insecurity about our seductive potential is tenuous, so we project these fabulous sensations onto whomever we are connecting with sexually. If we realized that, in fact, the choice and capacity to have that pleasure is actually coming from our own awakening body, we would save ourselves a great deal of emotional drama. Our attunement within ourselves to that sexual energy would greatly release us from dependence on the male. I am not speaking of self-stimulation, I am referring to the energy made available because of the body's final rush to entice us into reproduction. While the body's agenda is always reproduction, ours can be the wonderful feeling of so much energy that we can apply in many ways, such as healing and creativity. The resulting excruciating pleasure is nevertheless the same!

It is women who often love the marketplace scenario; we are natural buyers and sellers. We do it with our children, our husbands, and especially with ourselves. We always have an eye to promoting a successful facade. Until we let go, no one else can let go.

However, this can become a catch-22 because it is so easy to see everyone, whether our mates or our children, as a part of the marketplace. For example, mothers identify themselves through their children, so they become invested in creating success for them. Perhaps they buy them special toys or clothes or put them in status schools—"Put my kid out there first. My kid is going to be the star of the play"—because that is what gives them a sense of value. All too often there is a backlash from these tactics because children recognize when they are being used and go into passive resistance.

This externalization of self-worth prevents us from finding the very things we are searching for. Women say to men, "Why aren't you emotional with me? Give me your heart." But we do not know how to trigger the paths into those deep levels. We say, "I want you to show me that you love me." But we do not know ourselves what that looks like because we measure it externally by objects or favors.

This is a place where women manipulate. We want a man to show emotion, but we want it to be in our own code, which the man is supposed to decipher. We women need to look beyond our tyrannical Emotional Bodies and learn the emotional language and codes of others.

For example, one of the ways men give is by making love. They give the seed, the juice. But women often see that as a maneuver, as political. It is only political in the scheming mind of the woman. Women want the gesture of emotions, but we often are much less vulnerable than we pretend to be. We are not so open to going deep emotionally or spiritually with a person but instead are consumed with the "art of the deal."

We females are like the chameleon, always changing our presentation to avoid being caught. We are looking for what is attractive to the masculine rather than using the gifts we have. We are playing with the feminine powers, not really owning them. In sessions at the Light Institute, women are often shocked by the discovery that they make contracts and vows to get what they want and then try to change them as a new whim strikes. We are much more fickle than men.

We need to experience ourselves in new ways that will release us from the bondage of the marketplace. Entrapped in the buying and selling, we compete with each other, just as do men. Rather than competing, we must awaken compassion for our unconscious fears of being alone. Until we do that, we will be using men as ploys in a game we are playing with each other, rather than really loving them. We often do not really love our men. We use them; we still have a bit of that black widow syndrome. It is the illusion of identifying with the Emotional Body rather than identifying with the deep essence.

THE QUEST FOR BEAUTY

In the past, when a woman became older and had sacrificed everything and worked herself to the bone so that her family could advance, she was placed on a pedestal and greatly admired. In many cultures the amount she was able to suffer measured her greatness. A woman who put everyone else first was repaid with a special deference given to her unequivocally by her children and friends.

Today, children do not give honor to the mother for that kind of activity, though they often demand it. In the modern world the reward for martyrdom is often sarcasm and abuse. A woman has an opposite pressure put on her now to somehow maintain an ageless body, to stay within the marketplace as long as possible because her activities and looks reflect upon the self-image of her entire family. It is sad to observe the number of children who are embarrassed by their mother's appearance and actually go to great lengths to hide her, especially if she is over-weight. Being burned out or aging because of raising a family is simply unacceptable in the world of the marketplace.

Beauty has always been of great value, but now the quest for eternal youth has created a new kind of unanswerable challenge for women. Consequently we have become more and more obsessed by the pursuit of the facade. Since marriage is no longer a guarantee of lasting relationship, we are acutely aware that we are competing, often with younger women—and the odds are stacked against us.

But true beauty is ageless. It is not the absence of lines on the face, it is a radiance that emerges from a happy, whole being. Everyone recognizes that kind of energy and enjoys being around someone who is radiant. Often, when a person begins to meditate, do yoga, or otherwise alter the inner self, those around notice the change and comment on how wonderful or young they look. One of the most common responses from family and friends of those doing Light Institute work is how completely different and radiant their faces look after the sessions.

The alchemists of the past had techniques to create the illusion of fresh, vibrant youth. These were not masks or substances placed over the body to hide the tragic truth of age; rather, they were alterations within the body, commanded by the mind, that changed the molecular structure so that the presence of the body seemed different. The poised, radiant person appears eternally beautiful to others. In my book *The Ageless Body*, I teach some of those techniques for enhancing the life force energy of the body.

It has always amazed me to see truly beautiful women go unnoticed because they are so judgmental and negative about themselves that their self-image overrides the impressions of others. Self-denial and hatred for the body create a stress that reinforces the attention on the exterior self rather than the inner source of true beauty. All of us have heard the axiom, "Beauty comes from within." Yet in this fast-paced reality the hope that our inner beauty can shine forth and be recognized will dim in the face of the need for acknowledged glamour, monitored by a self-absorbed public.

The promotion of glamour as an ideal has been truly a negative energy with regard to the self. Women try to pretend glamour by employing seduction techniques to cover up a deep-seated fear that they might not hold the interest of a partner. Perhaps half the fights and dramas within relationships are actually perpetrated by the subconscious need to ensure excitement. Thousands of couples around the world report that their best lovemaking comes after a fight!

The massive media invasion of our visual world sets the standard for the "skin deep" variety of beauty—so much so that we cannot appreciate anything more subtle on our own. The hitch is that we lose the ability to recognize beauty without outside confirmation. Such insecurity eats away at the roots of beauty as an art of expression and leads us directly into the wasteland of mediocrity.

Beauty is an absolute essential in life. It lifts the spirit, soothes the heart, and brings us smiles. Although it is true that some people are born with indisputably beautiful faces or bodies, everybody has at least one attribute that can be expressed beautifully. If we weren't seeking approval of others, we could have magnificent experiences expressing the beauty of our individual form.

The expression of beauty is an art form that could be of great challenge and amusement to everyone. It is a never-ending process of creation. You can look at the color of your skin or hair and enjoy mixing the colors of your clothes to constantly create a new look. All traditional cultures have spent time creating styles for the body that allow each individual to express the self or change the image through accent and whim.

In Western cultures self-assessment is even more crucial, as we may employ the advantages of technology to change our noses, our tummies, or our hair. This could all be great fun if it could be done with the joy of the quick-change artist rather than the grim determination of the somber body hater. There is nothing unspiritual about changing the body if it is done with the lightness of creative adventure. Like the child who tries on his father's hats and his mother's scarves, we all want to see how it would be if we were like this or like that. There is a tremendous difference between hating your body and choosing to enhance something because you think it looks beautiful.

If you choose to alter something physical about yourself, it is important that you actually ask permission of the body to undergo such a procedure. Your body needs to be assured that it won't be violated. When you learn to communicate with your body, it will delight you by performing in ways you never expected. It's so simple to converse with it just like an old friend. Tune in and be amazed by how it answers you with streams of color, pulses, electrical currents, and even words.

The pursuit of beauty needs to be a pleasurable exploration of color and contrast. Part of the reward for being in body is the joy of variety as it teaches you to become the designer of the self. Everyone has a vast repertoire of ethnic, cultural, and racial memories that function as source material for creative self-expression. If you can fathom that you actually composed your body from the other bodies you have owned, as well as from the genetic parents you chose, you will realize that what you look like is exactly perfect. Within the framework of your soul's experience, you are beautiful. As you honor *your* expression, others will find you fascinating and attractive. You must simply become brave enough to choose for yourself what is beautiful to *you!*

WOMEN AND THE ANCIENT ARTS

There are other ways to use the female body that can teach you how to have relationship with the self on higher levels. When your body can find communion with energies other than bodies, you will come into your own as the magical being you are.

The female body is particularly designed to be in concert with Mother Nature. In natural ways, it can receive information on profound spiritual levels about the natural course of events, the cycles of the moon, the purity of the air, and the currents of energy surrounding the earth; just to mention a few. The fluids in our bodies play a great part in this transmission of knowing. Just as water acts as a conductor of sound, these fluids seem to carry messages of happenings within the earth. Perhaps, because of the menstrual cycle, the fluids in the female body are constantly in flux and in concert with the ebb and flow of the earth's fluids. This has helped women in ancient societies find water or gold, for which they were held in great esteem and honored for their mysterious powers.

Sometimes these fluids are excited by the motion of energies moving toward an event even before it takes place, and this precipitates a precognitive awareness. Here is a real mystery, unsolved by science, yet still very common around the world. I experience these fluctuations in the body quite regularly. I call it "sloshing" because it feels a little bit like the water in a bathtub sloshing from side to side.

Though I always have had precognitive awareness, these "knowings" increased dramatically after being present during two of the strongest earthquakes (8.6 on the Richter scale) felt on the American continent. The first one struck in the early morning while I was having hot chocolate in the tiny kitchen of my *mamacita*'s apartment, which sat at the corner of a lovely park in Mexico City.

Suddenly I felt a kind of vile nausea rising up out of the pit of my stomach. There was a curious roar that increased in volume and pitch. As if in concert with it, people throughout the twelve-story apartment building began to wail as well. My *mamacita* lurched for the door frame as the building tilted in an almost unbelievable forty-five-degree angle out over the park. We were wedged together within the flimsy door frame, and I watched in mute fascination as long cracks appeared in the walls and the pictures flew in slow motion toward the huge round bay window that was now providing us a view directly to the ground. Listening to the sobbing prayers of our neighbors, I waited without breathing to be flung from the room.

Fervently we held fast to the door frame, and after an eternal nine seconds it was over. Had the quake been a vertical motion instead of a rolling one, the whole of Mexico City would have dropped to the ground. My body relived the earth's rocking motion for days afterward. Ten days later the entire scene was reenacted when an aftershock of almost equal magnitude struck again. The nausea overtook my body minutes before the sound began, so that I was already up and on the alert as the jolt tore through the building and opened a huge hole in the ground in front of the entrance.

I witnessed other earthquakes in Mexico, including one that devastated Acapulco and one that caused two skyscrapers almost to collide with each other. My body's awareness became more and more astute, so that I "knew" there would be a quake up to forty-eight hours ahead because of the sloshing in my own body. My little son, Bapu, recounted the same sensation to me at three and a half years old, just the day before a big quake hit Nepal. He said his tummy was bouncing and that he felt many, many people were about to die in the country with the high, white mountains. We sent light energy to help both the earth and the people.

It is so crucial to pay attention to what your body is telling you. In the temples of old, women were trained for years to interpret the complexities of the natural world as the subtle nuances presented themselves to those skilled enough to observe and read them. Passed down from all these wise women are the kernels of their knowing that are entrenched securely in your genetic makeup, if not in your own Akashic soul records. You can trust the whispers that come to you when you are still enough or truly care to listen to the timely messages pervading the universe at any given moment.

It isn't just an absurd thought that you might perceive happenings from across the planet or inklings of things to come.

These inklings are for the benefit of all and greatly enrich our individual lives as we realize that through these subtle avenues we can contribute to the world.

The time of the witch hunt is over. The fear of someone who seems to have an unexplainable talent is a dangerous throwback to the Dark Ages. It is true that the world has always feared women for their primordial mystique. Menstrual cycles, the power of birth, and the telepathic and emotional access of women have provided a shroud of mystery about the feminine that too many of us seek to exploit, mostly from our own lurking fear that we are not enough. That is a big one for women, pretending the mysterious and insinuating hidden powers of the feminine mystique without actually having to call them forth.

Nevertheless, it is part of the gift of your feminine body to discover any intuitive gifts you have and explore everyday avenues for their use. You can revisit these ancient arts through the streams of your consciousness and put them to good use in your life now. Choose the practice of predicting the weather, perceiving the molecules in the air, communing with plants. All these endeavors are worthy of your attention. All you have to do is let yourself tune in and be open to the answers you get. Perhaps you wonder how you can listen to Mother Nature in a big city, but let me assure you that if you can just extend yourself, you will feel a peace that you have never known before.

THE TRAP OF THE GODDESS

At present there is a move afoot to enhance the status and image of the female. It began first with the women's liberation movement, the male aspect of the female, which helped us be more assertive and visible. Now it has shifted to place the female on the level of the "goddess" as we have realized that being equal or even side by side with men does not seem to be enough. The goddess lets us feel special and untouchable. However, the truth is that we must get rid of the imprints of "less than" so that we do not have to play the game of "more than."

Women do not need to be the goddess *or* the man. It is enough to harness the spiritual energies and impregnate the world with that knowing. In times past, priestesses lived separately and devoted their entire energies to such pursuits. They were rarely focused on daily life. It is now our challenge, yours and mine, to reclaim those capacities and apply them in the midst of daily chaos. Let us not daydream about old rituals, but rather put the power of consciousness to constant practice in everyday life as we call the rain or sun, send healing energy to others, or influence the politics of nations by our inner meditational focus.

We are spending a lot of time these days getting together and creating rituals to give more strength to our intentions. We become dependent on the presence of each other and the symbology of our acts to confirm that what we are doing is special. This is because significant doing is relatively new to women, who erroneously feel that their family lives are not important enough. Women love ritual because so much of who we are lacks form and structure. Ritual is a way of expressing the formless through some kind of insinuated code so that the female can find an avenue of action. But this is really an appeasement of the pain of invisibility because so much of our inner experiences cannot be expressed in form. The self-worth of a man does not depend on subtleties that he may or may not access (depending upon the male/female mix within him). But we women, in physical body, hunger for the ease and comfort of structure. We want to show what we can access, measure, and touch. In the past a woman could turn only to her family to somehow try to show that she had created something. Women have tried to realize their value through the structure of family, the structure of emotions, and the surrounding of the self. This has become a dilemma today, as less and less value is given to the woman in the home. As a result, we women are rushing into the job market so that we can be acknowledged for our creations.

We need to let go of the glamour attached to being recognized as someone "special" and get about our work! In all the countries where I have lived, the most powerful sorcerers and healers have been virtually indistinguishable from anyone else except to the initiated eye.

This is not the time of the high priest, the high priestess, or the individual will. This is the time when those natural faculties of the feminine, the inclusive faculties of cooperation and merging, have great value and can actually change the course of history. Instead of creating more separation by attempting to make up for lost time and become special, women must realize it is time for them to be the teachers who can show men how to use the feminine energy, how to access tenderness, how to sit in the still void and create something out of nothing. Teaching how to look within for the peace that must precede any true action dissolves the stress that fills our energy field and causes so much of the world's prevailing aggression.

TRICKS

We don't need to pretend or play tricks on ourselves or others to get what we need. Sometimes it seems that the plain stuff is just too boring for us and we are not happy unless there is a twist, an innuendo, a variation on the truth, to dress up our reality.

One of the most common tricks on the self is the drama of the victim. We will rarely admit to wanting to be alone, so we will arrange for the man to leave us. We will create a reality around us that frees us from taking responsibility and at the same time makes us appear to be the "wronged party'" or the good guy! This is a subconscious game that is uncovered as we explore ourselves deeply. It often comes as quite a shock when we realize that we were seeking relief from the relationship but didn't have the courage to do it. If your mate is pulling away from you, it is time to meditate deeply on how you are contributing to it. It could even be that it is a balancing of karma whereby you need to experience the results of deception. Don't treat it as if it were his fault, but rather as if it belongs to you; then you can clear it from your body and it will disappear. Since your body holds all experiences, emotions, and thoughts, you must find the residues within it to clear the patterns so that they do not reoccur. You can learn to identify these negative patterns of your Emotional Body and sweep them away as if they were crumbs on the table. These tricks and many more are in the way of our true power, so let's just clear them now!

Take a deep breath and close your eyes. Ask your body where it is holding deception or manipulation, expediency, emotional tricks, or even the ego. Search for each of these individually. When your body answers by giving you a sensation or showing you a place, or you hear a word, take your consciousness into that part of your body. It might be your heart, uterus, left knee; it doesn't matter where it is, just let your body express it to you. Then, simply ask the body what color it needs to dissolve these habits. Draw the color into that part of the body until it feels full.

If you do this conscious exercise each time you catch yourself engaging in tricks, you will become a powerful and happy being!

THE MOTHER TRAP

Perhaps the strongest hold anyone has on another is motherhood. I don't think it is an exaggeration to say that our tie with our mother is never outgrown, but that we project it onto many relationships throughout our lives. This can become a phenomenal weapon in the battle to maintain the upper hand in a relationship. Although the honor once bestowed on the mother has largely disappeared in today's world, we still have a subtle recognition that we wish our mother would take care of us, that we could return to the womb.

We women often use mothering as a hook, even a seduction,

to hold a man to us. This technique precipitates a nasty payback of karmic retribution because the man may turn out to be weaker than we are. We may have used the mothering enticement to attract him, then ultimately feel furious that he cannot protect us or help us as we had wished. All the gratification of winning is lost because what we really wanted was for him to subdue or overpower us. It is a tragic trap.

Everyone secretly wants to be mothered. For men especially, the sense of being mothered channels them backward into childhood, when they could connect with their feminine energies. It is a grievous but common pretense for women to insinuate that they will give mothering and then not give it, or extract indebtedness in return. Often they make a great show of serving or fussing over others in a motherly fashion and then expect that something will be given in exchange. We women too often are counting up all that we can extract from someone because we have given them some solace. We are famous for our hidden agendas that go undiscovered by our dependent prey.

However, executing our hidden agendas requires a tremendous amount of energy. We often feel great resentment that our children and husbands do not give us enough, when in fact it is we who are wasting our energy trying to maneuver them into giving us what we want the way we want it. We feel that we give too much or that others drain us of our energy. There are always certain people who make us feel tired just being around them. This is because both of us are trying to suck energy from each other, which is exhausting.

These are the tugs-of-war of the Emotional Body, which is always weighing and measuring. The Emotional Body cannot reason or say why it is tugging and pulling in this way. The mind can say why, but the Emotional Body can only say "How much? How much am I giving you in relationship, and how much are you giving me?" It always keeps tabs, though the way it does this is not through accounting, but more through a sense of feeling.

The truth is that no other person can fill the void in your energy field. When you are exhausted, it is because you have

been using your limited e
tional Body. It is usually
deserve it, I am not wor
you are thus drained,
do it with anyone wl
allow yourself to re
though you might
the world, you w

It is so help
feel a lack of nu
support, or comforting yc
without limitation. Love matures
the Inner Mother. Calling upon her un
help you remember that the key to fulfillment is
of abundance. Unlimited, unconditional love comes on,
the source. The freedom of the giver is euphoric when it is
unshackled from the tether of return. If you can give and let go,
you will experience a godly sensation of true power and master-
ship in life. Once you are willing to tap into your own source,
you will truly become the giver. Only then can you give or take
unendingly in a relationship because it is not based on the response of anyone else; you become free.

We create boundaries by the role definition of our relationship
to each other. Sometimes the programming of "mothering" calls
for you to feel that you must force things onto others, such as
food, advice, or affection. When they do not receive it, you
become fearful because your sense of identity is based on their
acceptance of your mothering. You are using them to establish
safe boundaries for yourself. We depend upon those kinds of
boundaries all the time in order to be safe in relationship. That
is what is called karma, or reality by relativity; you be the child,
I'll be the mother, and then we'll both know how it will be
between us. Ultimately we must outgrow the limitations of these
stilted kinds of relating.

Today, there is a new problem cropping up in which mothers
are returning to work very early after childbirth. The new mother

FEM

168 •

needs six weeks to cle
energy discharging f
itself by returning
back to work. U
often stem fro
she is losin
and thus
place.
She
var

r the profound releasing of all the old
m the body as it simultaneously renews
its nonpregnant state. It is unwise to hurry
ortunately, the motives for this hasty return
the Emotional Body. It is as if the mother feels
ier identity as an individual person in the world
shes back to reassure herself that she has not lost her
onetary factors are a big part of this decision as well.
rs that she will lose her job, which adds anxiety about a
future. This kind of contraction actually inhibits future
ssibilities.

We must realize that the future cannot pass us by. Indeed, we are the center of our own destiny. Childbirth makes a woman more valuable in any environment she later chooses because it is one of life's most powerful teachers. The woman who has birthed has passed an initiation that makes her stronger and more able to cope with chaos, arbitration, and appreciation for another's point of view.

You must let go what you have outgrown, so that you can move on to the next octave of your life. Good job positions are not won exclusively through toil and clinging to your place, but more often by learning manifestation skills. By that I mean meditation and visualization about what you want and declaring your intention for better and new avenues of expression. Job status is directly related to salesmanship. What do you think you are worth? Probably a lot more than you dare! Work on your self-worth and your enjoyment of challenge. After mothering you should be able to get a job that delights you. You will have begun a journey into the mechanisms of what motivates people. If you can work with a two-year-old or a six-year-old, you have the psyche of the world in your hands.

It is a matter of switching your focus from the fear of outside approval to internal clarity of intention. Never make do at work because you think you are unworthy of something better. The skills of orchestrating a family definitely translate to performance in highly complex job situations. You might explore how many times a day you mediate emotionally based upheavals, and you will come to realize the value of the skills you are learning, in terms of the world outside. The reverse holds true as well—if you treat your family as if they were your colleagues at work, you will be infinitely more successful at home.

More and more couples are choosing not to have children or are unable to reproduce. The capacity to nurture is not lost, however, even though the hormonal support for nurturing is not present. The memory passed into the body by the parents and, even more important, the multi-incarnational imprints are more than enough to allow a loving and genuine expression of mothering. We can turn to our pets, husbands, friends, and even the world to open the flow of this magnificent energy.

Today there is a great opportunity for us to allow the natural flow of subtle energy to expand out and to feel the freedom that is available, because our identity need not be based on success as a mother completing the biological mandate, or in the home, or as the wife of someone else, but, rather, on the multifaceted energy that has learned the mastery of alignment. The art of attunement creates channels of communication that are urgently needed on the planet today. Because the masculine force hasn't the vision to choose life over the lust for power, we women, as natural visionaries, must step forward and participate in global choices. Our stepping forward creates the balance that is so badly needed in the world today.

In order for us to maximize the power of our wisdom for leadership, we must become true friends with each other. Our capacity to cooperate and foster relationship is greatly needed in the global arena. Rather than competing, let's discover how fabulous it is to embrace a relationship that uses our psychic connection, our capacity to feel deeply, to accompany each other through life. This is not the "misery loves company" fellowship so common in women's groups, but the coming together to support our capacity to see beyond the walls of frustration and depression onto the levels of wisdom and purpose that lift us out of martyrdom. It is the major task of females to become the teachers of the feeling state, to use the Emotional Body, not as protection against loneliness, but, rather, to give ecstasy and wonderment to the human experience. We can teach each other to bring what is deep inside, the wisdom held in the heart, out to the world with dignity and indisputable power.

Our true power is not over each other, but in the spiritual realm. Up until now all religions have been controlled by men and thus focused on the doing. This has led to religious wars and the dogma of structure, as men have sought to define the form. The evolution of life must come from being, which carries our awareness into the divine hologram. It will be difficult for us because there are few role models. We will have to become the manifesters and join the yang reality to this end. However, the force behind the manifesting will come from access to the source.

9

IGNITING THE
FIRE$ OF FU$ION

We have by now come to grips with the principles of fusion in terms of the magnetic force that brings opposing and relating forces together. We have glimpsed the dynamics of the energies that ignite the spark of that fusion, whether it be people or emotions that we resist, honorable opponents, or the essence energies within us, seeking reunion. We can go further and explore those catalytic elements through the practice of exercises that stimulate fusion to take place.

When we want to ignite the fires of fusion, we have to begin with the whole being. Only a whole being can experience fusion with another. Otherwise it is simply the back-and-forth motion of one person approaching the other and then the energy disengaging, rather than two whole energies merging together in a way that precipitates the fire of a new kind of relationship, a new kind of energy that is born of the fusion of the two.

The perfect place to ignite the fire of fusion is within the physical body because it carries the sacred spark of energy that is necessary to interface with the third-dimensional world. The body's unique physiology is responsive to the electromagnetic waves of other bodies, which are mutually stimulating. This external sensitivity begins in the chakras, or energy centers of the body, and can be shared or amplified through exchange with a partner (though a partner is not at all necessary to ignite that spark of energy because all crucial elements reside within each being).

Within the self the consciousness must come into a state of expansion so that it becomes aware of itself within a universal medium. It may be focused through the mind on physical cues or on the blending of physicality with pure, spiritual essence. As this energetic field moves out, it feels itself fluid enough to extend into any spatial concept, to create communion and fusion with the self and all that is.

However, there is a complementary energy between the male and the female that facilitates fusion because of the energetic attraction between them. The creative force, Mother Nature, has designed it this way to stimulate the memory of the one, which took place at conception when the egg and the sperm united. In fact, conception is the best example of fusion. With these primordial imprints, is it any wonder we feel driven to merge together?

When the energies come into contact with each other, whether that is the self in communion with universal energies or the communion between two people, there is an incredible motion of energy extending out and being drawn in, which magnetizes the exchange or the spark. This is the pulse of life that is repeated throughout the cosmos. People often describe this experience as a tingling sensation or a thrilling vibration all over the body. The body feels light and exhilarated. I call this the Shakti Body because "Shakti" is the word used to express the pure life force energy.

AWAKENING THE SHAKTI BODY

If you can awaken your Shakti Body, you will have a whole new relationship to youself and to any lover or partner you might have because your energy for fusion will be so much greater. This is not difficult to accomplish; anyone can do it. It just requires some practice to teach yourself this new energetic awareness.

Let me show you an exercise for fusion that will help you get in touch with the energy flows necessary to merge your yin and yang energies within yourself or with another person. But realize that first you must be firmly seated within the center of your whole being so that you can allow the natural flow of energy without impregnating it with emotional need. You can do this exercise by yourself or with another person. When you do it with another, know that the spark that takes place is created between two whole energies that come together. One does not absorb the other, yet each being draws in. You and your partner each draw in what is germane to your own physical, emotional, mental, and spiritual bodies.

You will be doing the exercise with your breath to help you follow the energy. It is important to practice this motion alone initially to master it. Later you can use the circuitry of another person to feel yourself extending the energy out and bringing it back in.

Here is the exercise.

If you are a man, you should breathe in through your open mouth and exhale by consciously following the breath going out through your genitals, the first chakra. If you are a women, you must do the reverse—breathe in through the vagina and extend the energy out with your exhalation through the mouth.

In using the mouth, you are taking in the energy that feeds the heart, which automatically allows the energy from the first chakra to rise up and consecrate merging through the opening of the heart. By extending the breath out into the realm of manifestation, you create an energy around you that you then pull in.

It is this rhythmic pulse that creates balance. As these source essences are stirred from their innermost repositories and begin to flow outward, the yin energy rushes out to meet the yang and the fire of fusion is lit. This makes for a perfect balancing because the yin way of giving comes from the upper chakras, whereas the yang way of giving comes from the sustaining of the force, through the source chakra.

In the past, you may have identified with a certain pattern of energy flow, whether the yang genital or the yin mouth, so you might not feel much when you practice moving the energy in the opposite patterning direction. But you can use your Higher Mind, which is the will, to direct the energy: "My intention is to draw energy in here and to extend it out there." As you start to trace the pattern of energy with your will, the body follows your intention and creates the flow. Within your body is the memory of the energy going in the opposite direction because you have both male and female in your repertoire. You must awaken the memories of both energy flows—the yin and the yang, the receiver and the giver. Once you can do it in the pattern that is natural for your present gender, you can practice going in the other direction.

So now, switch it around and do it the opposite way. You must be able to move, at will, these cycles of energy in both directions. If you are a woman, push down as if you were giving birth. Push down and out, then inhale as you take in through the mouth.

During the sexual act, it is crucial for the female to give the juices to the male that excite him to give them back. It goes from her to him, to her. She must begin to be able to move the breath, the fluids, and the consciousness down into that area of the body.

If you are a man, visualize drawing the juices into your genitals and up through the heart and extend out through the mouth as you exhale.

It is important for a man to learn to draw energy up rather

than extend it out because it opens his heart and makes the connection between the heart and the physical energy.

Just allow yourself to feel the energies going one way and then the other way, like a Ferris wheel.

Moving in both directions creates a balance between the male and female inside you. With one person you may play the male or the father, with another the female or the mother. That explains why, with some people, you are the one giving and giving, whereas with others you may be the one who receives. You take it in over here and give it off over there. When you become aware that you are selecting these things, you can change a relationship that is entrained in a particular direction and take it in another direction. This allows the other person to align with you or move away. You become the master of reality by becoming the master of energy, karmically finding the balance.

As your consciousness focuses in both places, the drawing in and the sending out, you find a perfect merging and balance. You will also notice that your ability to take in is not dependent on an outside source, such as another person. You can still take in and draw up energy even if you are not practicing with a partner. One of the reasons women feel energized after making love is that they are drawing in energy, whereas the man is spending it. This exercise will help tremendously to rebalance so that men can discover what it is like to feel energized after lovemaking, too! When the man reverses the cycle at the end of orgasm, a revelation of experience is available to him and his partner, since it is then that the convergence of body and spirit occurs. This drawing up created the motion we are looking for to alter and quicken the energies in and around the body.

When you are practicing this exercise with another person, there are two energy flows that must go in opposite directions in order to create complementary energy together. A figure eight of infinite energy is created between you, like an unending spiral. This is different from the Ferris wheel energy pattern you experience when you do the exercise by yourself.

Experiencing the figure eight is like making love with the Divine God Self. As it goes in and out, it is beginning to clear the energy. It often feels hot as it comes up because you are accessing the yang force in you. You are drawing it up instead of extending it out. So when you are taking this yang blood energy, or chi, of the physical form and drawing it up instead of expending it, you are activating all the living energies that are related to being in form. This stimulates the Emotional Body by passing through the solar plexus.

Thus the heat rises, which creates enough energy to radiate power. As you give off energy, it expands and cools. You will notice when you do this little exercise that the energy may be warm next to the body, but when you get the auric field out touching your fingertips, it will often be cool, rapidly vibrating energy. Each body has its own rhythm. You don't have to deliberately feel that one is out and one is in, or that one is cold or hot. These are all just ways of helping yourself be able to experience so that you can control and attune the energy.

When the consciousness is able to perceive this and do it in tandem, the capacity to know another person is complete and the Emotional Body is fulfilled. It is merging or fusion that brings such great ecstasy to the Emotional Body—to be in concert, in relationship, so that we do not merely think about what the other is doing but experience it through our capacity to align perfectly with another, to surrender even the breath, to move together with another being. Surrender does not create emptiness. Surrender creates fullness because the confines of the separate self dissolve and the energies merge together. Once you have glimmered that each being in your presence can respond and mingle with you on these spiritual levels, you can experience the simple bliss of touching.

It is thrilling to experience the fluidity of altering your focus to match that of another. For example, if you begin with giving, it creates a space for receiving that is more than you could ever have received before. If you are not saying "Oh, I don't want to be the one that gives it all," but are focused on the inhaling and exhaling of the energy, you are creating the current of ecstasy.

If you do the fusion exercise during the sexual act, you won't be able to tell whether you are the male or the female because the energy is moving in both channels. The willingness to match the cycle of the other is what creates the tremendous vibration of energy that allows for an effortless merging to take place. Profound bliss follows this merging, and it is not dependent on mutual orgasm. It is dependent on nothing more than the ebb and flow of energy that becomes effortless as the consciousness attunes to its pulse. When that happens, there is no longer any separation. You can change your cycle at will to create a blending that does not acknowledge or even remember the confines of separating. When you focus your intention on giving yourself these kinds of experiences, you are tapping in to an energy that can be used in infinite ways, including synchronization of sexual exchange so that two people who perhaps were not compatible physical partners can become so.

If the consciousness of one of them is able to embrace the whole and use that cycle of giving and receiving, of extending and drawing in, then each intention, each effort, each experience with another being, has the potential for complete fulfillment. Every individual creates his or her own octave of response that is sourced inside the self, then shared and extended through another. Thus the figure-eight cycling can go on within one body or two bodies or multitudinous bodies at once.

In this scenario the body is not merging because of need, it is merging because of fullness. When you then encompass an-

other person, you are not absorbing them. There is a big difference between taking from someone and simply passing through
them. What happens, energetically, when you pass through
someone is that you are able to caress all the energy that is
complementary. In other words, you are extending out and that
person is taking in. You come into alignment with each other,
and that is what creates that little flip in the figure eight, so that
it simply amplifies the energetics of both. When that happens, neither one is aware of the weighing and measuring: "Am
I giving you more than you are giving me?" As that falls away
the Emotional Body becomes ecstatic because it experiences
source.

When you surrender totally, sexually and emotionally, and
you are not holding some part of yourself back, you have the
unlimited sense that the confines of the individual self merge
with the universal. This is the moment of "critical mass." There
is so much more than you could ever take in, and you are
immediately filled with the energy that creates the ecstatic spark.
Your heart goes to the absolute maximum that it can take, like
listening to a sound that reaches the highest pitch before it explodes. Often, when the Shakti ignites, it blasts you onto the
universal level and you fuse back to your Divine Source.

The more that you use the feminine energy, the more emotionally, physically, and spiritually you amplify your capacity to
direct energy so that you become the great giver. The power of
the feminine is to become the unlimited giver. You are simply
a channel of energy that is coming in and going out. Then all
avenues of reception are open, and this is when the fires are
ignited—when there is no closure, no resistance to receiving. As
you practice this flow of energy, you lose the fear of separation,
so that when the energy recedes, you know that it is simply the
breath that creates an expansion for the next exchange, the next
merging. Thus you dissolve fear.

THE FUNNEL OF INITIATION

The moment you become the giver, you cannot fight with your lover, your mother, or your father because, suddenly, whatever you are wanting from them—which is definition of the self—dissolves. They cannot give it to you. You are too big.

This is called the "funnel of initiation," when you suddenly realize that you cannot get what you want from someone else, that their interpretation of who you are is not big enough to encompass all of you. That is when you have to let go of caring about someone else's judgment, you stop holding back your love or your truth. You are no longer afraid to speak, and by the same token, everything that you speak becomes beautiful.

When you experience such all-encompassing energy, the consciousness does not perceive the personality self. That is the moment in which you truly see God, in which you can dance in the energetic fields, delight in the sparks of the constantly changing energy.

Once that pulse has been activated within the physical, sexual, and emotional bodies—through the heart, the mind, and the spiritual energies—it creates a reverberating, ongoing patterning, a pool into which you can dip at any moment when you are willing to let go of the limitation of the self. Each time you choose that quality of energy, the auric field stands charged because the very energies that create the will and the substance of life have come into complete relationship to each other. When you give yourself that gift, the charge in the energetic field stimulates it in everyone else around you. This is the Shakti, the life force energy that can be passed like a chain of ignition, in every direction, in every octave, to every being!

One of the greatest gifts of being in body is the potential of sexual energy to link up with the cosmos as you flood yourself and your beloved with delicious sensation and love. The consciousness expands beyond the sensual level, beyond the pleasure of the stimulus, because the motion of expansion allows mind, pure mind, to enter. It is mind that creates. However, you cannot *think* yourself into those levels of energy. You must use your energy field to feed back perception, which then creates the stimulus to expand beyond the locality of any part of the body or the body itself. All these definitions simply dissolve.

The Emotional Body sets these standards of limitation, and then the nervous circuitry of the physical body follows suit. "I can only take this much pleasure," is the thought just before you shut down the feeling. That is why it is important to start with the simple awareness of giving and receiving, which amplifies the energy. The sloshing effects get faster and faster as all the cells become ignited. They become ignited electrically, biochemically, and magnetically.

Then there takes place a merging with all life force energy. You can have orgasmic experience with a tree simply by practicing these energetic flows. Just do this thing inside you: inhale, exhale, inhale, exhale, and pretty soon the Shakti Body starts tingling with energy that spreads out.

The sexual currents do not stop with orgasm. They provide the sustained space to have God experiences. This is what I have called "cosmic orgasm" in my book *Ecstasy Is a New Frequency.* Cosmic orgasm is bigger than the electrical currents of the body, so it shoots through all the chakras and opens them. The rush of energy becomes the ongoing flow of the subtle bodies making love with the cosmos. It does not stop. The rush simply opens the aperture, the gates, through which you follow the energy. The taking in and the giving out will start to move in both directions, continuing to build until one body cannot hold the frequency and the cosmic explosions echo outward, dissolving the self.

As you become full, and you expand the circuitry of the energy, you are activating all the chakras. The Emotional Body moves up into cosmic levels. The illusion of separate bodies dissolves, and the feelings naturally rise up onto universal, divine levels because you are touching. The point of reference of touching is coming from source.

The Emotional Body that has lived within the frame of reference of the third-dimensional world, the physical body, or the mind body suddenly is able to come back to its source. It returns to that sense of being divine. In the face of the divine is the fullness that dissolves projection onto others. It creates a change in the Emotional Body that never can retreat completely back to measuring "But what am I getting here?" When you measure, you get stuck, you interlock. This is karma, the relationship of need. As the Emotional Body approaches the universal octaves, it experiences that by giving—it is full. The levels of need and projection, the levels of defense and fear—all dissolve.

As you practice this Shakti exercise you will begin to feel what it is like to not hold on, to rush out beyond the self and trust the flow of life to bring you what you need. Holding on to anything creates congestion that causes great discomfort and ultimately forces change. This congestion is a great gift that precipitates the ignition of the fire of fusion.

DANCE OF THE UNIVERSE

Fire transmutes so that what was once the yin becomes the yang, and the yang flows back into the yin, creating the dance of the universe. It is a Möbius strip, infinite energy, that never concludes, never finishes. As soon as there is critical mass, it explodes and then it goes in the other direction.

This is a clearing process, creating a balancing within you that profoundly alters relationships. You will discover that you can come together with anyone outside you in a very, very different way. You do not need them to be a certain way because you become aware of what energies are at play inside yourself.

For example, one of the major difficulties people have on a sexual level is that one person may be very physical sexually and the other person is not. He may be very physical and she says, "That is too hard. You are not sensitive enough." Maybe he has no sensitivities, could not even dream of what foreplay means.

When he comes on with this hardness, she could use her feminine energy to teach him to feel what he is missing. His consciousness may be caught down in the lower chakras, disconnected from the heart. It is only the lack of heart that is causing him to thrust too hard because he is trying to get to something of which he has no consciousness. She says, "You do not know how to make love to me." And he says, "What is she talking about?" He cannot hear her. He cannot understand that she does not mean "You are thrusting too hard." She is really talking about the fact that she is looking for a physical connection that expresses the tenderness of the heart. She is hungry for an emotional exchange that will occur through a physical one.

But she must lead the way by giving him what she is looking for herself. She needs the feminine energy and all the sensitivity it entails. When she can find it within herself, she can give it away and it will therefore come back to her. If she gives him the heart, it will fill the hole in him that causes him to push so hard. Then all of a sudden he will begin to expand and experience his own heart, which he will share with her.

It is a kind of recognition. As you feed the self, you become abundant. When you meditate on what you most need, you can begin to fulfill it within yourself. This adds to your mastery because you now can be the source of energy. That is what mastery is—the source of energy.

The feminine energy embraces energetic laws that have to do with the capacity to extend, expand, and receive because it is the drawing in by the feminine that creates change and brings the energy full circle. Ultimately, it does not matter if you receive or give because you receive as you are giving, especially while making love. You stop measuring it because you are the universe.

BACK THROUGH THE ARC OF FORM

The whole attitude of lovemaking is magnificently transformed when a man who accesses the woman within himself can make love, truly make love, in the way that all women deeply desire—not with the thrill of being conquered, the game of submission or seduction, but with the experience of merging from the physical, back through the arc of form into the vast reaches of the feminine psyche. Here we are attuned to all sensation, all nuance, and all the essences that so heighten the experience of life.

There is a complete and utter difference between a man who makes love to conquer and a man who surrenders to the blending of energies. As our consciousness expands in this way as we clear the limitation of cultural imprints, as we recognize the purpose and power of sexual energy, lovemaking will go into an entirely new art of expression.

Throughout the ages, great emphasis has been placed on the technique of lovemaking, so much so that we have completely lost the essence, and like bodies drugged and numbed, we have almost lost the way into the inner reaches of our interpersonal psyche. But the sensitivities that are available to someone who is using the consciousness of all the body's knowings is immeasurably greater than a body locked into the male or female stance, unable even to dream itself a part of the universe. As our consciousness expands in this way, as we clear the limitation of cultural imprints, as we recognize the purpose and power of sexual energy, lovemaking will go into an entirely new art of expression. It is evident that both men and women are seeking this now.

Women must teach men to go beyond release by surrendering themselves to the deepest level of merging, without demanding from their partner. A man who has outgrown the hunger to conquer can surrender to the blending of energies.

When men learn to make love as if they were women, and are able to use a level of consciousness that can feel simultane-

ously the feeling of the other, not only will we have reached a
new octave of communication, but the result of those experiences
of merging will even create a new kind of child being born—the
child of merging, the child of fusion, will never be polarized,
neither in body nor in personality, to one side or the other, but
will have the benefit of each, amplified by the act of fusion.

10

FREQUENCIES OF CONSCIOUSNESS

The frequency of our consciousness is not limited by our karma, by our actions, or by the weight of our Emotional Body but is directed only by the intention of Higher Mind, which is the aspect of consciousness that can stretch beyond third-dimensional reality, if contacted. Through the power of the Higher Mind, we can easily go from the depths of despair to the heights of ecstasy. Though we have felt that we are trapped in our physical bodies and emotional dilemmas, or bogged down in our daily realities, all of these things can be erased instantaneously, brought forward, or remixed through the power of the focus of the Higher Mind. They are energies that are not foreign to us but are the gift of our presence in these bodies.

Through the biochemistry of our bodies, not only can we alter the heart rate and blood chemistry in the brain, but we can also alter the auric field and thus the frequency of the Emotional Body, so that virtually any octave that we choose to embrace is available to us, solely through our intention. As we practice our intention, the clarity of our will, we begin to come into contact with frequencies that alter our perception and our experience of reality. All matter begins with a thought carried into form by the will. It is the soul that gives permission for it to manifest; and thus we have the need to commune with the soul through the expansive frequencies of the feminine energy.

CHANGING THE FREQUENCIES

In order to learn to move the frequencies of your consciousness, it is necessary to commit the self to sit in the presence of your own energy field. By becoming familiar with your subtle energies you can then alter them effortlessly by consciously brushing away any debris and crystallizations through the use of breath, color, sound, and self-compassion.

If you begin your meditation by spinning, you will stir the stagnant energies in and around your body so that they literally spin off you, and when you sit down afterward, you will feel the energy clearly moving off your body so that you have a reference for your auric field.

One of the easiest ways to access the light of consciousness is through the breath. Breath attracts prana, which is that sparkling energy surrounding all living things that looks like pinpricks of light. A pranic breathing exercise will build up the charge in the body and make it more natural for you to meditate on yourself as a being of light.

Breath slowly and deeply, imagining the multicolored fibers of your auric field radiating out from you. As you inhale you draw in the prana, activating the light of consciousness within the body; as you exhale, you remove the toxins from the body. Notice any glitches and, with detachment, simply use your will to smooth out and release them.

This is where choice begins. By paying attention to this emanating energy, you can alter any place in it that is stuck so that it becomes smooth and strong.

The physical body and the subtle bodies have whole systems of energy that facilitate heightened frequencies of consciousness and intermingle with each other to quicken the current of life. The nervous system has its relay of impulses jumping across the synapses to carry consciousness throughout the body. The quality and frequency of those impulses are influenced by the subtle Shakti life force energy that moves inside and around the nervous pathways. There are also the meridian channels that harness energy flows, as well as the large channels of blood and lymph that move the fluids through the body.

All these different moving energies must come into concert with each other in order to hold the new frequencies of consciousness. The rapid-fire energy of ecstasy is so explosive that the nervous system must be taught how to elongate this high ecstatic pitch, lest it fall back into its opposite of despair. In my book *Ecstasy Is a New Frequency*, I talk about the actual pulsation of ecstatic energy that moves from the excitation of ecstasy into rapture and then into a sustained bliss, so that there is an alchemical pulsation that maintains a level of responsive integrity. If you want to be able to maintain these states, you must lay the foundation.

It is so easy and direct to ask the body what color it needs to quicken these frequencies. As you draw that color into your body, you feel the change. Light is a loving way to dissolve negativity. Disease, negative emotions, or scar tissue all create a dullness or darkness in the body because there is no movement of the chi, or energy, whereas the presence of light reinstates motion and unleashes the blockage that brings about a new balance. It is that simple.

Sound is the yang channel for altering energy because it has the potential to interrupt or take over the pulsation of all the tissues in the body. Sound can even destroy matter, so it must be used only in concert with the body's mandate, not chosen arbitrarily by the mind. The sound I recommend is humming because it accesses the actual vibration of the electrons in the cells. One of the most powerful meditations I know is to attune to the atoms of your cells and then copy the sound. One day it may be a high pitch, while on another day it may be low. This allows the evolution of the body to take in the hologram of all of the particulates that may be thought forms, biochemistry, light frequencies, and pulsations. All these universal energies come together within the hum. The hum allows for all the divergent radiant energies to commune with each other, creating an integrity that assists you in moving in and out of time and space. Humming maintains the frequency of the physical body in a heightened state, yet an integral one.

ENTERING THE UNMANIFEST

Usually the first thing that people experience as they enter the unmanifest realities is a profound shift in their perception of light—as has been reported in the near death experience and the death experience itself. This happens because energies are filled with essence, life force energy, prana, and light.

The moment you let go of the particulate, individual separate self and experience the self, not as physical body or as emotional feeling, but as consciousness, you become the source of knowing. That is the feminine force, the knowing, the potential, that can move freely in any direction of choice. The light that pervades cosmic levels is the essence of consciousness. When you sit in the center of consciousness there is a radiance, a radiance caused by the incredible charge of life force that begins to pulse out around you. When you become aware of radiance, that there is radiant energy coming from you, you are able to perceive radiance everywhere.

The individual self surrenders and flows into the whole. That is the direction of the feminine energy, to merge, to unite, to include—to include all radiance, all presence.

When you sit in the center of consciousness, you can articulate the hologram of life so that all the experiences and potentials present in the hologram are equal. The frequency of radiance does not separate the negative from the positive. There is simply life, which is divine! The Shakti energy carries the spark of light that creates the body and flows through all the subtle bodies as well. The feminine Shakti nourishes and feeds the purpose of life, the karmic intent that allows the soul to grow. It is the Shakti that stirs the Kundalini energy. The powerful Kundalini awakens at puberty and represents the potential of creation and procreation. If it is not dissipated at the sexual level, it can thrust upward to trigger enlightenment.

USING THE ENERGIES

There is no person who cannot activate and use, or even master, these various energies. By simply following the thread of consciousness into the experience of ecstasy or radiance, the force of the energy will show you how to become a part of it as it shapes and reshapes purpose and articulates form. All you need do is meditate on the essences of the different energies. Can you imagine how it will alter your life if you spend your energy contemplating joy, ecstasy, or the sense of radiance?

Meditation creates the space for the alteration of consciousness. It brings you to the center, the still point of the universe. You are there. It is not the same as reaching up for something outside of, in front of, or above you, but it is something that is part of your true self. Time dissolves as you sit alone in these frequencies of chi. You do not wonder what is next or what you will have ten years from now, because you are totally fed by what you have right this second. Consciousness is limitless. It never ends.

ACTIVATING ECSTASY

A good exercise to teach yourself about different octaves is to ask your Higher Self to show you the frequency of ecstasy. If you ask and then sit in a receptive meditative space, the body will begin to attune to ecstatic frequencies that allow universal energy to be drawn into you. The moment you meditate on ecstasy, you will not be able to view your separation. You will go right into the pure energetics and essence of consciousness. Every time you ask, you will have an experience of ecstasy.

Each time you call forth ecstasy, it will penetrate you differently. Your body will experience it in a different place or be stimulated by a slightly different sensation or current because it has literally trillions of ecstatic recordings from many lifetimes and dimensions brought on by its infinite experiences of form.

Each energy, each frequency of consciousness, is itself a threshold to another level. For example, when you open yourself to ecstasy, it will result in an increase of radiance and you can become aware of yourself as a radiant being. You can experience the recognition of the energy radiating out, and you can witness the radiance activating your ethereal, Light Body.

Ecstasy is a kind of spewing radiance, and that is why it is so hard to sustain. If you recognize it as an initial charge for expansion, and then focus on the centering still point, such as the hum of the atom, there follows an integral consciousness that makes it safe for the Light Body to become activated without losing connection with physicality, with the third dimension.

The ethereal body, the Light Body, is formed by the coalescence of light energies that reflect the soul. The interface between the subtle bodies reshifts so that the Emotional Body begins to feed from the light, rather than limit the light, because as it feels expansion and freedom, it loses its memories of aloneness and separation. As the consciousness reaches the octaves available in the Light Body, the electrochemistry of both the physical and emotional bodies are altered and you experience the merging of self and soul.

Through the very frequencies of light that come together, your light body is illuminated and coalesced into form. There is a great healing to the third-dimensional body when you nourish yourself through the light body. The physical, mental, and emotional bodies are given a much needed respite from anxiety and overstimulation.

When you begin to work with your light body and all these incredible frequencies, it is important to be gentle with the physical body because the excitation of the nervous system through the *nadis*, which are channels of energy, and chi is so great, it can shock them. The body must be protected with rest and fluid so that as you bring the purity of those radiant energies into you, you do not create a cleansing too strenuous for the physical body's nervous system.

Meditative repose is what protects the physical and emotional bodies and allows for this quickening. It is that point of center in which the self recognizes the capacity to move back and forth from the manifest to the unmanifest without confusion, because it is in touch with the radiating center.

At the Light Institute, as we comb through the Akashic records and clear away the limitations of emotional residue, the experiences of radiance and divine bliss emerge. The unembarrassed recognition of lifetimes in which you have been able to access these radiant frequencies, this powerful chi, quickens and lifts you higher onto the path chosen by the soul. Do not be afraid to acknowledge yourself and to use your consciousness, to call forth ecstasy, or to use the energy of radiance; they belong to you!

Children do this all the time. The child is unabashed to become ecstatic, to experience radiance and to play with it. We can play with it, too. It is ours. Children do it not because they are innocent or young, but because they are so old; because they are still connected with higher energy. They have a tremendous store of unlimited energy for running and jumping because they are still accessing the radiance that brought them into body. The child does not have to say what it is but just accepts and responds to the currents that are everywhere.

By calling forth the Inner Child and asking "Show me the energy of ecstasy," you will get flickers of colors or dancing sparks of light or giggles, or something that represents ecstatic frequencies to you. Once you play with radiance, all of your control and limitation and incapacity to quicken simply dissolve in the face of the thrill of expansion.

All you need to do is give yourself permission to let go for just a moment. Initially you will be able to soar into the higher ranges of consciousness only for brief flickers of time, but each experience will create a base from which you can build so that it is easier and easier to return. Focus your intent and practice the exercise: "Okay, I am going to sit in a meditative space, and I am going to ask this energy to come. " Perhaps one day it is asking for ecstasy, another day it is feeling radiance. Each time you do it, you build a vocabulary that begins to insinuate the matrix of the personal self back through all of the particulates of karma, the Akashic records, into the whole of the universal soul: all that you are or ever have been become fluid and whole.

Ecstasy communes with fullness. It is like a mysterious Möbius, figure-eight energy that circles around encompassing you and yet is ever expanding and evolving outward. Ecstasy is a more yang energy than other radiant states, such as bliss, because it is so exciting to the nervous system. Like a man and his orgasm, ecstasy spews out energy until it is spent and the pendulum swings back, often creating a momentary backwash of depression or doubt because of the emptiness that ensues. The Emotional Body will then take over the pull because of its fear of being annihilated. As you expand, the little self goes through the same kind of dying that the body experiences as it passes through the funnel from the third dimension into the universal energies. You can either become aware of the rapture or let the Emotional Body plummet you down. However, this emptiness is the opportunity to fill the self with higher vibrations, and there is always a choice never to return to the lower levels of existence.

Each time you focus on higher energies, you free yourself from those slow vibrational planes considered the realm of the adult. Thus, it is not just the child but the whole person who is connected with these frequencies.

The electrical quality of ecstasy can be harmonized with the body by amplifying the liquidity of its pulsation. Fluid is the amniotic sea of the feminine energy. It is the unfathomable source of transcendent knowing. Learn to use the rocking back and forth that is the feminine pulsation. It is spiraling upward constantly, swinging in and out, merging the male and female.

The excited levels of chi stimulate all the energies in the body and open the channels for "cosmic orgasm." Cosmic orgasm is the rush of electrical orgasm felt in the genital stream, magnified a million times. When it happens, every cell of the trillions of cells in the body is ignited and seems to explode with the charge of energy. It rarely happens during the sexual act with a partner but will occur at the most unexpected times, being awakened from sleep, for example. It happens spontaneously when the body is totally open.

Each time you use the will and give yourself permission to perceive, you reach higher and higher octaves. The dimensions of reality expand and become more subtle. Communication with life explodes into channels of recognition that break the barriers between species, between all of nature. At this point you are entering the world of the magician, the genius, the saint.

You can commune with the dolphin, the birds, and the stars by tapping into the vast sensory repertoire that is beyond the ordinary, sleeping human awareness. Through the mechanism of the old brain, you can revisit the genetic memory of the evolutionary patterns and perceptive capacities of all the beings who have come before you.

In the future we will recognize that this is not only an experience of spiritual enrichment, but may well carry vital survival secrets for our species as we deal with environmental hazards that have placed us in jeopardy but have already been surmounted by other ancient species.

Through the use of the feminine spiritual energy, you can perceive what the bird knows because you have evolved from the brain of the bird, as well as that of the insect, who has highly developed survival skills. Many such gifts are available to us on the evolutionary ladder. Let yourself explore beyond the human repertoire that so entraps you within the narrow alleyways of your limited mental body.

The third eye is the gift of the human. The third eye accesses holographic knowing. It "sees" and thus gives articulation and definition to essence. This is the knowing energy of the feminine, in the spiritual sense, that shapes essence into form.

At the Nizhoni School we have identified more than seventy senses with which to touch life! The sense of delight, of sensuality, success, of radiance; all recall the divine. Attunement to the seventy senses is an exercise of consciousness, an exercise in radiant frequencies of enlightenment. As you explore the vast sensory array, the self dissolves. If you can feel or know what the bird knows, you are no longer the particulate. You are no longer caught within the separated human unit. The exercise of perceiving senses goes far beyond the limitation of pleasure or pain, far beyond the five senses. As you harken the sixth sense and slip through the veil of matter, there follows an incredible explosion of consciousness as you engulf the universe.

Enlightenment is simply the inclusion of all that is—the universal knowing. It does not require struggle, merely surrendering to that still point of the center that is the capacity of the feminine. It is really just a process of acknowledgment. By doing simple exercises of allowing yourself to commune with these universal frequencies, you are bringing the whole universe into your own center. As you do that, you begin effortlessly to manifest the full potential of human consciousness.

The feminine octaves are the octaves of spirit that set aside the urgency of the physical and emotional bodies by bringing you into contact with the higher potentials, the potential for ecstasy, bliss, and rapture, rather than judgment, limitation, and fear. As you begin to speak the language of the feminine energy, the awakening energies course through you and you can learn to shift these octaves of consciousness at will. When you step into the unmanifest worlds, reality does not rest upon the small or the particulate; it expands miraculously to include infinite variety and delight.

For example, try this exercise.

Draw an electric blue line in front of you, and intend that when you step across that line, you will step through the threshold into the higher octaves. Now, feel yourself move forward as if you were going "Home," were reaching out with the essence of your being to embrace your soul. Just step across and see what you perceive.

Whatever you perceive there will quicken the chi of your being so that you can hold those energies until they become truly a part of your life. Here is the pivotal point, the threshold to the expansion of consciousness—*your* choosing to bring form out of the void, to shape nothingness into something that can interact with you and give you energy simply because you have allowed relationship. As you transcend the human arena, you are bathed in a radiance that far exceeds human love or awareness but which can help you to root it here on earth.

It is, literally, going Home. Because the Higher Mind continuously receives signals from "beyond," it knows you are referencing Home. You draw the line and say, "I am going to cross over into the unmanifest." It does not mean death, as the Emotional Body thinks; it means becoming included in the universe.

We all hunger for that inclusion, which is the feminine energy. It is the mothering principle, sprung forth from creation. The creative principle is not just the masculine force shaping form; it is sourced in the ecstasy of creation that precedes it. The feminine knowing, unformed, comes first. Then the ecstasy of the knowing creates the fire, the fire of fusion that moves out and creates the form. That is the dance of the male and the female, the yin and the yang. Only when they surrender to each other do they merge and transcend into ever-spiraling enlightenment. Feminine fusion is the surrender that opens to the receiving, that expands the arc of inclusion!

All we have to do is say "What is the sense of this energy?" and we can access it. You do not have to try. Anybody can do it.

By sitting in this space of peace and expansion, your energies are quickening and you are accessing those frequencies of chi that have enough power to pull the formless into form. The mind has begun to shape and identify so that what was only essence can now be materialized. Through this definition of form, the mind participates in altering reality. The body verifies and confirms this with the help of the seventy senses. It interacts perceptually with the form and responds to myriad stimuli. You may feel as if your whole body is buzzing because of the electrifying quality of multidimensional response. It is fantastic!

Let me give you an example from one person's view through the "Window to the Sky": This woman's first foray across the line came in the form of a white unicorn that brought sighs and tears as its very presence created a new balance to her feminine expression. The unicorn has always been symbolic and sacred. Although it issues forth from unseen worlds, it is itself a yang energy whose horn symbolizes its ability to pierce the veil. Its magical image cues the mind that it has entered a higher realm. The unicorn is like a bridge. It spans the space that separates yin and yang, essence and form. The woman felt uplifted by a spiritual presence that she could identify and at the same time be encompassed by such a new and powerful energy that prevailed in its presence.

Once when I crossed the electric blue line, I perceived a sort of sweating sensation coming from my third eye in the middle of my forehead. It had the lightness of dew yet the cohesiveness of sap and the sweetness of nectar. It literally slid down to bathe my eyes, yet I simultaneously experienced it at the back of my palatte, spreading a divine scent that passed down my throat.

Across the cosmic threshold, psychic and perceptual senses merge in incredible ways so that you might taste a color or smell something you see. Whatever you perceive will stimulate a copying effect on the part of the cells and thereby offer you the gift of a new potential. As you grow, the quality of the ecstatic states you attain will be ever changing, for there are many levels of consciousness, or enlightenment.

All great truths are simple and experiential. No reality that is holographic can be held within the limited conceptual field of the finite mind. Rather, all that you call forth from the unmanifest void awakens your capacity to be one with the universe and, therefore infinite. Practice with the energy of radiance.

HUMAN FUSION

As we poise ourselves for the next millennium, we must reach to the horizon of human consciousness in order to see our species safely on to the future. Environmental, political, and economic circumstances will make it necessary for us to begin the resolution of merging together as global citizens, one family of humanity.

All the awareness we have gleaned in our personal struggles will see us through the collective themes of global magnitude. They are little different from the hopes and fears of the individual who agonizes over how much money, power, or acknowledgment will be given. The issues of food and energy shortages, international domination, and upcoming environmental crises are but the vehicles of our awakening consciousness. War is obsolete, coercion an old nightmare of the child. Today and tomorrow we can accept only our own choices.

Inherent in every choice is the mirror of the self in which we must seek to find the face of Peace. Through these common dilemmas, we will ultimately come to recognize our option to face the challenges of existence—together! We will soon see how incredibly powerful we are in group.

One of the highlights of my Peace Corps days was to watch the dawning of this realization on the faces of people in tiny villages as they discovered they could do things as a group that they would never dream of doing individually. I am not referring to the mass mentality in which people seem to descend to the lowest common denominator and act out negative emotions in group situations with the pretense that they are honorably in pursuit of a cause. Rather, I am speaking of the selfless dedication by which individuals melt into a new, integral entity with such one-pointed focus that manifestation of their intention flows easily from their endeavors.

Today we have the option to communicate our needs around the world and seek resolution from the vast storehouses of wisdom present in the minds and hearts of our numerous relatives, each of whom has adapted to life in ways that can instruct us all.

It is thrilling to see citizen diplomat groups springing up around the world that are actively seeking a role in solving international stalemates by bringing humanity together. As people of different areas of the world begin to dialogue, we can perceive that our goals are not so different and that cooperation is a major asset in attaining them. This is the theme of the next millennium: cooperation, merging, fusion of energetics.

No longer can we afford the luxury of allowing governments or other special-interest groups to represent us unequivocally in the affairs of our planet. It is not enough to count on them to see to our best interests or protect us from danger. Neither is the smug comfort of blame an emotional or political option anymore. You and I must see to our needs by acknowledging our mutual complicity in all global events, large or small. The margin of error is diminishing at an alarming rate, so that our participation is mandatory for the future.

If you can realize how your interaction with the outside world reflects what you are learning on the spiritual level, you will grasp the importance of contemplation and reflection as a resource for action. Using the feminine energies to perceive the hologram will give you the edge necessary to make the right choice.

You may ask what you can do to change the world. Any significant change must come through the transformation of your self and how you commune with those around you. Every such effort to work with others on any matter, whether it is business or child raising, brings you closer to human fusion. Translation of spiritual realities into daily life requires training the consciousness to observe the flows of energy, perceive the auric field, and put your intention on transcendence, that vertical shift from one level to the next. This path moves unwaveringly toward full human potential, not indulging in the pretense that anything outside the self is designing your destiny. At all costs we must not surrender to the excuse of separate realities. What happens in Africa, India, the Middle East, or the Soviet Union affects us all and calls upon us, a sacred response.

It is crucial for us to remember the purpose of all the present chaos and to focus steadfastly on the solutions that remain locked in our awakening consciousness. In every octave of experience the old habits of human existence are being torn away—not because we are less than we once were, but because our collective value systems must be internalized so that we can live them without the prodding of external force. There will soon be a great turnaround in terms of individual quality of life as we each design it from our unlimited source.

While our financial and societal systems are in for big upheavals, people around the world will begin to use their experiences to forge new values and new meaning from the most adverse of circumstances. Humans have always had the capacity to reach each other across the barriers of catastrophe. This is the part played by Mother Nature—to help the swaggering *Homo sapiens* find their place in the infinite universe by demonstrating the relativity of power.

It seems a mysterious course of events that in every place we create strife and violence, nature mimics us with an earthquake, volcano, drought, or other catastrophe to force us to cooperate and acknowledge the commonality of our existence. She seems determined to match us at our worst and impress upon us how puny are our displays of self-importance and illusions of species dominance. World economics, health issues, and even the search for the stars are beginning to bring us together. Our human bond offers us the only viable support to withstand the future tests of our own cosmic design.

The future taunts the face of the past. We must be careful to look to our manifestations, lest they cast shadows on our options. Each of us has an obligation to expand our individual repertoire of requisite variety so that we can orient ourselves in the global stream. We each have multitudinous talents and predilections to guide our path and help us feel fulfilled in life through our unique contribution.

We have explored all the patterns and roles of the play through our projections and programs instilled in us by family, culture, and the breath of history itself. Now we have the understanding and the tools to set us free. There is a little cosmic joke by which we have been afraid that freedom would spell loneliness, and thus we have clung desperately to the past. The truth is that freedom will bring us together in much wider arcs than the old separation by clan concept that has so long divided us. Hopefully, we have finally recognized ourselves in the entrapment of separatism that has placed us on this present precipice.

It is an almost unfathomable leap to release the others in our life from being responsible for our sense of happiness and fulfillment and to go on to discover that all we need is inside us. Life is a ceaseless process of growth. There will always be the coming and going of relationship. Therefore, when relationships end, they can end with grace. If you outgrow the boundary of a relationship, your partner has the freedom to expand with you, leaving behind the contracts and limitations of yesterday. At any moment you can choose to explore together completely new forms of communication and relating.

There is nothing more profound than praying or meditating together while you are doing what otherwise you would do alone. Making decisions, for example, is exceedingly more powerful if the Higher Self is brought forth. Including spiritual expression in daily activity is sublime, especially in a comfortable, natural way with friends, partners, and family. Even if you do not have a partner, close spiritual communication satisfies a great deal of the human dilemma. It is an integral part of conscious living as it enters into all our expressions, both in our outer and inner worlds. Spiritual communities will increase around the world because the path to enlightenment is so much fun together.

We will rediscover words like "devotion" in more joyful context. Devotion is the discipline of intention. We will apply it to manifest new societies and extended families, devoted to each other on soul levels and willing to contribute with all their faculties to the good of the whole.

We have never used spiritual energy as the base of relationship, society, or existence itself. We have been too focused on emotional or physical survival. Now we have begun to evolve to a point whereby we must recognize that without the connection with the source, life itself has very little meaning. In today's complex world, we simply cannot continue to scavenge the peripheries of consciousness without rounding the bend and coming back to the still center of the spin.

I predict that in the future people will come into relationship and spend entire lifetimes together—totally differently from what we do now. The word *commitment* will take on a whole new meaning, with no vestige of the defiance, drudgery, and denial we enact through our present understanding of it. We still hear the word as a mandate to give, rather than as the joy of offering. Instead of a boxed-in feeling, commitment will refer to spiraling arcs of passage, continually extending relationship into the realm of bliss. In the future, our commitment will be to the joy of the soul in communion.

Delving into the power of the feminine feels like spiritual initiation to us, but it is a familiar world to our children. It is imperative that we leave it intact and not strip them of the most profound gifts they have to meet life. The magnificent sensitivities of the child are the guardians of human spirit.

Even birth itself is finally being recognized as a sacred event. As I wrote in my book *Ocean Born, Birth as Initiation*, we can use this most primordial experience to merge with each other and become ourselves the passage to life.

As a result of my poignant experience of giving birth in the sea, I felt the power of birthing as a tool for global consciousness. I began the Birth for Peace project to facilitate other birthing families to use birth as a message and reminder of our global citizenry. Now, you can choose other countries and places on earth to give birth to a child who stretches the web of human family. As we bond together in these profound expressions of life, we become free of the boundaries that belittle our magnificent future.

Within the upcoming years, as life takes on new meaning, we will reinterpret our goals as parents and teachers of the souls incarnating to join us. If we exemplify the integration of the masculine and feminine, we will no longer produce little girls and boys who secretly wish to be "the other." In the light of spiritual determinism, it will become a most honored event to bring forth the next generation. They are the more enlightened ones who can show us how to have it all. Teaching these "teachers" will make the art of teaching a fascinating sojourn into human consciousness.

The Nizhoni School for Global Consciousness is a prototype for the future because it demonstrates the integration of multidimensional reality. The students of its Global Business School can be comfortable and effective in diverse environments because they are so comfortable with themselves.

While the students at Nizhoni's Academy of Ecology and Energy are learning about the environmental atrocities inflicted by our shortsighted greed, they are also able to seek answers stored within the mind of the cell: Mother Nature knows how to cure herself and us. These are fantastic lessons for human consciousness.

There is a new awareness that will rescue us from the pit of darkness in which the intelligence plunges to the level of disuse, bound by the imprints of cultures and societies that have been created for the control of the individual. Intelligence is suffocated by the illusion that we are only the children of our parents, students of our teachers, and flocks of our churches. We must break the bondage to the wheel of karma that fixes us to that desolate repetition.

Recognition of spiritual resources is a new awareness that will rescue us from the pit of darkness. It is spiritual awareness that will intercede in the chaos of the world. Through the grace of the feminine energy we can accept the truth that we are each our own teachers, our own healers, and that our innate wisdom will withstand the test of life. The Higher Self waits to carry us into our Light Body, heralded by a new epoch of human consciousness sincerely willing to embrace Peace.

Feminine fusion, the merging of all opposites, is the force of Peace. Peace comes when there is nothing lacking or desired. It is the embracing of all there is, beyond judgment, beyond separation, because it revisits the Source. Though it is full, Peace is not stagnant; it moves in the arc of evolution. It is awake and conscious.

As we commune through the energetics of the feminine, we come peacefully into the knowing of the self. As we embrace the recognition of each other, an inevitable attraction stirs itself into the fire of fusion. Human fusion is at hand. We ourselves are the only solution to our present dilemmas: you and I are the goal of the quest.